EDITING
THE
COMEDIA

Edited by
FRANK P. CASA
and
MICHAEL D. McGAHA

 Michigan
Romance
Studies

MICHIGAN ROMANCE STUDIES

Vol. V, 1985. $9.00

Managing Editor: Floyd Gray
Assistant: Sally Silk
Typesetter: Trudy A. Driscoll

Michigan Romance Studies is a serial publication of the Department of Romance Languages of the University of Michigan. Each volume is presented by a guest editor and focuses on critical and literary subjects of current interest in the various Romance Languages. Publication in the series is by invitation only.

All correspondence should be directed to *Michigan Romance Studies*, Department of Romance Languages, University of Michigan, Ann Arbor, Michigan, USA 48109.
European Distributor: Librairie Nizet, 3 bis, Place de la Sorbonne, 75005 Paris, France.

ISSN: 0270-3629
ISBN: 0-939730-04-9
Library of Congress: 81-50963
Copyright 1985 Michigan Romance Studies

PREFACE

During the century spanning roughly the years 1580 to 1680, Spain produced one of the greatest theaters the world has ever known, claiming a place of honor alongside Periclean Athens, Elizabethan England and the France of Louis XIV as one of the cradles of drama. Rich in poetry, fable and insights into the human condition, Spain's Golden Age theater counts as one of mankind's most notable achievements. Nevertheless, while the painstaking work of innumerable scholars during the past century has enabled us to know the other great theaters of the world—the works of Aeschylus, Sophocles, Euripides, Shakespeare, Racine and Molière—in a state closely approaching the original, Spain's dramatic masterpieces continue to be misunderstood and neglected. Attempts to analyze and evaluate the works of Lope, Tirso, Calderón and their contemporaries, or even to translate or perform those works, will be but a fruitless effort as long as we know the plays only in editions prepared hastily, carelessly, and with little regard for the texts penned by the author or even those used in the original performances. As the few reliable editions produced in recent years make evident, there is no more urgent or rewarding task confronting the Hispanist today than editing *comedias*.

The Spanish *comedia* looms before us as a vast unexplored territory. Only a minuscule fraction—the tip of the iceberg, so to speak—of Spain's dramatic masterpieces has been seriously studied, and even that tiny sampling of important works has often been misunderstood because it has been isolated from the context of which it formed a vital part. Furthermore, the characteristics of a few well-known but not necessarily representative plays have given rise to unwarranted preconceptions and generalizations, resulting in a distorted view of the *comedia* as a genre. The greatest damage done by these false stereotypes, so often repeated in histories of Spanish literature and even in specialized studies of the Spanish theater, has been to discourage our brightest young scholars from dedicating themselves to the study of the *comedia*. If the *comedia* were indeed the mindless, unquestioning repetition of dramatic formulae whose content consisted of a ritualistic manipulation of worn-out concepts on love, honor, religion and government that our textbooks so often describe, it would hardly merit our attention. In fact scholars are only now beginning to recognize that the *comedia* accurately reflects the teeming diversity, intellectual ferment and social tensions of the milieu that gave it birth. This discovery is due not in short measure to the patient work of those editors who have dared to depart from the inherited orthodoxies and to let the *comedia* speak for itself.

It is our hope that as these recent developments become better known, more young scholars will be inspired to specialize in *comedia* studies and the Golden Age theater will regain its place as one of the most important branches of Hispanism. The editing of a *comedia* is at once the best possible initiation to the complexities of the Golden Age theater and the most valuable service a *comedia* scholar can contribute to his chosen profession. Unfortunately, graduate departments of Spanish have up to now offered little encouragement to would-be editors. Seminars in textual criticism are almost nonexistent. Successful editors have lacked a forum in which to share the benefits of their experience with others. Most first-time editors have begun their work by imitating the characteristics of the best editions known to them. Nevertheless, every *comedia* is unique, and the methods used in editing one may be inappropriate for another. What is needed—and what we have attempted to provide in the present volume—is a theoretical introduction to the fundamental problems of the art and science of editing the *comedia*.

Textual criticism as practiced today is a method which has evolved through a long process of trial and error. We can learn much from both the accomplishments and the mistakes of our predecessors. It therefore seemed to us worthwhile to preface this book with the late Arnold Reichenberger's survey of the history of *comedia* editing, originally published in *Editing Renaissance Dramatic Texts: English, Italian and Spanish*, edited by Anne Lancashire (New York: Garland, 1976), and reprinted here by permission of the University of Toronto Conference on Editorial Problems. Reichenberger observes that a major reason why so little progress was made in the rigorous editing of *comedias* until relatively recent times was that earlier editors, faced with such a vast profusion of texts, succumbed to the temptation to make as many as possible of those works quickly available to the public, disregarding the fact that mere quantity could not compensate for the scandalously mutilated condition in which they presented those texts. Beginning with Juan de Vera Tassis and moving down to Vicente García de la Huerta, Eugenio de Ochoa, Manuel de Rivadeneyra, Marcelino Menéndez Pelayo and Emilio Cotarelo y Mori, the efforts of these editors have ranged from the ambitious to the monumental, yet in most cases they have given us versions more plagued with errors and misunderstandings than the already woefully inadequate seventeenth-century editions on which they were based. It is no wonder that many nineteenth- and twentieth-century *comedia* scholars, whose knowledge of the works in question was derived almost entirely from badly defaced editions, accused Golden Age playwrights of a sloppiness and lack of attention to structure which were in fact more often the result of bad editing than of bad writing. Even Reichenberger, careful scholar that he was, did not reject these fallacies. Recent scholarship has cast doubt on the contentions that Lope de Vega was the "genius of conformity" and that the *comedia* was a collective enterprise—both so confidently asserted in Reichenberger's article—yet his earnest call for a more scientific approach to the editing of Golden Age dramas is still worthy of our attention and is in fact the *raison d'être* of this anthology.

One of the first Spanish scholars to give serious thought to the problem of editorial procedures was Marcelino Menéndez y Pelayo. In the "Observaciones generales" preceding his edition of the *Obras de Lope de Vega*, he established what may be considered a hierarchy of reliability for texts: 1) autograph manuscripts; 2) editions issued by the author during his lifetime and under his direction; 3) copies of manuscripts prepared by reliable persons; 4) theatrical scripts or copies made by amateurs. Menéndez y Pelayo recommended that autographs be printed as they appear, making sure that all changes, corrections and erasures contained in the manuscript are pointed out. In the case of the second group, he felt that the author's wishes should be respected even if they conflicted with the manuscript. After all, even after writing the final copy, the author reserves the right to change his mind. Only if the changes were forced upon the author by someone like a censor would the original copy take precedence over the author's express wish to make a change. In the case of copies of manuscripts, care has to be taken that the transcriber has not assumed the right to make "corrections" on the manuscript. As far as the last alternative is concerned, copies made for the theater or by amateurs, the Spanish scholar recommended the strictest scrutiny in order to avoid the introduction of alterations in the text.

The case of the single extant manuscript leaves the editor no alternative. He simply has to accept the limitations imposed upon him by the circumstances and make only unavoidable corrections: words that are evidently wrong, incorrect attributions of dialogue and re-establishment of proper versification, not by inventing new verses but by marking the missing lines with periods. All of these sound suggestions which coincide with many modern editorial practices were unfortunately not followed even by Menéndez y Pelayo himself. He rightly pointed out that Alfred Morel-Fatio had needed two volumes to publish his edition of *El mágico prodigioso*, will full editorial apparatus, an effort that could not possibly be repeated in the edition that he was preparing.

Be that as it may, the ground was now prepared for a systematic approach to the editing of Golden Age plays. While it is not the task of this short introduction to give the history of editorial changes and amelioration of practices, it is just, nevertheless, to recognize the contributions made to the field during the last fifty years and to single out, if only representationally, the names of C.A. van Dam, William Fichter, Joseph E. Gillet, Diego Marín and Arnold Reichenberger for their outstanding efforts.

No single reference book could possibly contain all the background information an editor will need in preparing a particular edition. We have tried in this volume to provide a starting point, focusing our attention on issues which face almost every *comedia* editor and which are at the same time of fundamental importance. The five distinguished editors who have contributed articles to our anthology have themselves chosen the topics to be addressed, and each one has written on the aspect in which he feels most competent.

In his essay on the editing of texts in multiple versions,

William F. Hunter lays out some general principles for the setting up of stemmata in order to recover or reconstruct the earliest ancestor common to all versions. He warns us that it is not the purpose of textual history to arrive at an absolutely authoritative text. Nor is the setting up of stemmata a self-contained activity. Errors in a text may derive from a variety of sources, ranging from speedwriting to revivals of plays, from cuts made by authors to theatrical adaptations, from illiterate copyists to deliberate cuts by *suelta* printers. In setting up stemmata, one seeks to classify variant texts according to genetic groups which are determined not by shared readings but by shared altered readings. In setting up groups, it is important to remember: 1) that manual copies create variants, so one copy can be distinguished from another; 2) that the bulk of a text is transmitted unchanged, so copies retain features of all their ancestors. Above all, Hunter warns us to be modest and realistic in our expectations, no matter how conscientious and serious the effort has been.

The possibility for errors in the transmission of texts is multiplied by the editorial conditions and practices of the period. Don Cruickshank introduces us to the chaotic world of the printers of the Golden Age. To begin with, he reminds us that plays were printed only when impresarios saw no further possibility of making money out of them in the theater. The gap between the writing and the printing was always considerable. Publication occurred only after the text had been tampered with because of professional exigencies.

A critical aspect of book printing was the long-standing scarcity of types in Spanish publishing houses. This circumstance resulted in the practice of casting off in setting up new galleys. This cannibalizing of earlier galleys in order to set up subsequent ones gave rise to a whole series of consequences that the careful and knowledgeable editor can utilize to uncover not only errors but cities of publication and even the identity of printers. Thus, a thorough acquaintance with these conditions, as well as the knowledge that there was a marked decadence in the standards of printing due to poor quality of paper, poor ink and worn types can be valuable investigative tools in the tracking down of a printed text and in anticipating sources of errors. Once again, the author warns us that, however useful this information may prove to be, it cannot replace a thorough knowledge of the playwright's works and literary practices.

It is precisely the all-important problem of versification that serves as the focus of the articles by Victor Dixon and Vern Williamsen. Both insist on the distinctiveness of the polymetric nature of Spanish Golden Age drama and see in the practice an opportunity for critics to unravel certain types of editorial problems. Dixon reminds us that meters were used with specific purposes in mind—purposes that were related to setting, characterization, intensity of action or states of mind. Authorial practices in these matters are often idiosyncratic, and these peculiarities can be of considerable aid in the establishment of a text. Williamsen recommends that a more detailed study of versification, and not only the presentation of raw data, be included in a scholarly edition. The study of versification habits is of inestimable value, since it can support claims regarding both the paternity of a work and the date of composition.

All of this docmentary evidence can be enhanced by the testimony adduced by the staging of plays as reflected in stage directions. The use or non-use of stage machinery can establish whether the play was meant to be performed at court or in a *corral*. John Varey discusses not only the possibilities offered by implicit or explicit stage directions but also how the circumstances of performances may affect the evidence present within the text.

Finally, just as important as the general discussion of topics is the long list of practical suggestions that each of the authors offers to the reader. While some fields already have well established editorial policies, especially under the direction of major publishers, editorial practices for *comedias* are still disturbingly uncertain. One recognizes of course that *comedia* editions are directed to various and disparate groups, but it still possible to implement many decisions that would bring not only a measure of regularity to the presentation of texts but also more reliability in the texts themselves. We hope that this initial effort will be of immediate help to colleagues who plan to prepare editions and that it will stimulate further interest in the discussion and codification of editorial practices that will, in turn, bring about more trustworthy texts.

Frank P. Casa   Michael D. McGaha
The University of Michigan   Pomona College

CONTENTS

PREFACE

ABBREVIATIONS

Arnold G. Reichenberger 1
EDITING SPANISH *COMEDIAS* OF THE XVIITH
CENTURY: HISTORY AND PRESENT-DAY
PRACTICE

William F. Hunter 24
EDITING TEXTS IN MULTIPLE VERSIONS

D.W. Cruickshank 52
THE EDITING OF SPANISH GOLDEN-AGE
PLAYS FROM EARLY PRINTED VERSIONS

Victor Dixon 104
THE USES OF POLYMETRY: AN APPROACH
TO EDITING THE *COMEDIA* AS VERSE DRAMA

Vern Williamsen 126
A COMMENTARY ON 'THE USES OF
POLYMETRY' AND THE EDITING OF THE
MULTI-STROPHIC TEXTS OF THE SPANISH
COMEDIA

John E. Varey 146
STAGING AND STAGE DIRECTIONS

NOTES ON THE CONTRIBUTORS

ABBREVIATIONS

BCom *Bulletin of the Comediantes*

BH *Bulletin Hispanique*

BHS *Bulletin of Hispanic Studies*

BRAE *Boletín de la Real Academia Española*

CH *Crítica Hispánica*

HR *Hispanic Review*

JHP *Journal of Hispanic Philology*

MCV *Mélanges de la Casa de Velázquez*

MLA Modern Language Association

MLR *Modern Language Review*

PBSA *Papers of the Bibliographical Society of America*

RABM *Revista de Archivos, Bibliotecas y Museos*

RBAM *Revista de la Biblioteca, Archivo y Museo del Ayuntamiento de Madrid*

RF *Romanische Forschungen*

SB *Studies in Bibliography*

TCBS *Transactions of the Cambridge Bibliographical Society*

EDITING SPANISH *COMEDIAS* OF THE XVIITH CENTURY: HISTORY AND PRESENT-DAY PRACTICE

Arnold G. Reichenberger

PRELIMINARY REMARKS

Ladies and Gentlemen. Please allow me to recall to your mind some basic data about the theatre of the Spanish Golden Age. The Golden Age or *Siglo de Oro* in general extends from the 1480's with Juan del Encina and ends in 1681 with the death of Calderón de la Barca.

This span of two hundred years is clearly divided into two periods of roughly one hundred years each: the theatre before Lope de Vega, *el teatro prelopista*, from Juan del Encina to the appearance of Lope de Vega, and the theatre of and after Lope de Vega, the theatre of the *comedia*. Lope dominated the Spanish theatre of the seventeenth century; and his achievement, the Spanish theatre as we understand it by the term *comedia*, lived on even beyond the death of Calderón, the last creative dramatic poet of Spain. The one hundred years after Lope are again divided into two periods of about equal length, although the break is far from being as sharp as the one between the *teatro prelopista* and the *comedia*. The second of these periods begins with the appearance of Calderón around 1630. His most famous play *La vida es sueño* ("Life is a Dream") is dated about 1635, the year of Lope's death.

Now, a word about the term *comedia*. The plays are called *comedias* because, while not free of violent emotions, death, and elements of tragedy, they end with order restored. *Comedia* is usually and correctly rendered "drama" or "play". What Lope's genius achieved was far-reaching: he created what can be called a formula for the Spanish theatre. Within this formula, a play consists of three acts, averaging 1,000 verses each, and is composed in a variety of verse forms. The structure is free-wheeling, sometimes episodic. It seems that Lope, dramatic poet that he was, is often so completely carried away by the scene he is developing that he does not pay attention to its structural importance or non-importance; thus he may be called Lope de Vega, *poeta del momento*. There is a strong lyrical strain in him. As a matter of fact, he is one of the triad of Spanish poets of the seventeenth century, together with Góngora and Quevedo. Other playwrights have their own characteristics and with Calderón the *comedia* becomes, let us say, more stabilized, the thought content more philosophical along the lines of post-Tridentine philosophy and theology. Calderón is the recognized master of *autos sacramentales*, the religious plays performed in public (not in the theatres) each year on Corpus Christi day. Their characters are allegorical figures.

Now we come to the subject of this paper: editing Spanish *comedias* of the seventeenth century: history and present-day practice.

I. The Communication of the Texts to the Reading Public, 1600-1800.

A. The Printed Texts.

If we take the term "editing" in the modern sense, to mean editing with some degree at least of textual criticism, we can expect little "editing" in this period; editing is in general virtually synonymous with publishing. And a play can appear in print: (1) as part of a collection of plays by a single author; (2) as part of a collection of plays by various authors; (3) as a single independent publication, unbound, for which we use the Spanish term *suelta* (literally "loose", "not connected"), meaning *edición suelta* (separate edition").

Our main and absolutely indispensable source of bibliographical and biographical information about the *comedia* and its playwrights is Cayetano Alberto de la Barrera y Leirado, *Catálogo bibliográfico del teatro antiguo español desde sus orígenes hasta mediados del siglo XVIII* (Madrid, 1860). This catalogue has been reproduced twice in recent years (London, 1968, and Madrid, 1969). Since 1860, of course, many bibliographical studies for individual authors have appeared, above all for Lope de Vega, but as a comprehensive bibliography for the Spanish theatre of the Golden Age La Barrera's work has not been superseded.

(1) Collections of plays by a Single Author.

(a) Lope Félix de Vega Carpio (1562-1635)

There is a relatively limited number of such collections in proportion to the number of playwrights, yet one collection is outstanding for the number of volumes it comprises: the twenty-five volumes, called *partes*, of the *Comedias de Lope de Vega*. They extend in time and place from Volume 1, Valencia, 1604, to Volume XXV, Zaragoza, 1647. La Barrera (p. 424) counts 290 *comedias* in Lope's collected plays, 76 in the collections of various authors, and 37 in *suelta* editions, a total of 403 plays, plus a number of plays attributed to Lope but of doubtful authenticity. Lope himself, in two lists of 1603 and 1618 respectively, names 427 titles of which 253 have survived in manuscript or in print.[1] Morley and Bruerton, *Chronology*, recognize 135 *comedias* as authentic Lope plays and 186 of doubtful authenticity.[2]

All *partes* but two, XXI and XXIII, appeared in more than one edition, at various times and in various places. All of these

1. Hugo A. Rennert, *Bibliography of the Dramatic Works of Lope de Vega Carpio. Based upon the Catalogue of John Rutter Chorley* (Extrait de la *Revue Hispanique*, XXXIII; New York and Paris, 1915), p. 130.

2. S. Griswold Morley and Courtney Bruerton, *The Chronology of Lope de Vega's "Comedias"* (New York, 1940). There is a Spanish edition, revised by Morley (Madrid, 1968).

were known to bibliographers at some time or other, but many are no longer extant, and some also may be ghost editions. *Parte* I had the greatest number of editions. It appeared altogether fifteen times between 1604 and 1626: in Valencia (three times), Valladolid (three), Madrid (two), Zaragoza (three), Lisbon (one), Amberes (Antwerp) (one), Brussels (one), Milan (one). It is easy to see that so many editions constitute many problems for the textual critic.

(b) Pedro Calderón de la Barca (1600-1681)

Calderón's production compared with Lope's prolific output was relatively modest. He wrote "only" 120 *comedias* and 96 *autos sacramentales*. The basic edition of his *comedias* is by Juan de Vera Tassis y Villaroel (who calls himself *"su mayor amigo"*), and consists of nine volumes. The nine volumes appeared in Madrid, 1682-91, by Francisco Sanz, *"impresor del Reino"* ("printer of the realm").

Vera Tassis had predecessors, the foremost being Pedro Calderón's brother José, who issued a *Primera parte* in Madrid in 1640, *"recogidos y sacados de sus verdaderos originales"* ("collected and taken from the genuine originals"), followed by the *Segunda parte* (Madrid, 1641). *Partes* III, IV, V were published by others: III in 1664; IV in 1674 with a Prologue by Calderón himself; V —repudiated by Calderón — in 1677 in Barcelona (actually Madrid). The Vera Tassis collection, in turn, was reproduced by Juan Fernández de Apontes (Madrid, 1760-65), *"invirtiendo completamente el orden de las piezas"* ("completely reversing the sequence of the plays").[3]

There exist several one-volume editions of Calderón's *autos sacramentales*, printed before the first collection appeared, published by Pedro de Pando y Mier, in six volumes, and printed by Manuel Ruiz de Murga (Madrid, 1717). The next edition is that by Juan Fernández de Apontes (Madrid, 1759-60). It is nothing but a reprint of the Pando y Mier edition, with the sequence of the volumes completely changed.[4]

3. La Barrera, p. 336.
4. La Barrera, p. 58.

(c) Collections of Other Single Authors

There is no time and probably it is not necessary to enumerate the other authors who have collections of their own. I will only mention the enigmatic *Segunda parte de las comedias del maestro Tirso de Molina, recogida por su sobrino don Francisco Lucas de Avila* ("collected by his nephew") (Madrid, 1635). It contains Tirso's most famous play, *El burlador de Sevilla*, the Don Juan play, but also many plays of doubtful authenticity. Tirso himself says in the Prologue that four plays in this volume are not his, but he does not say which.[5]

(2) Collections of Plays by Various Authors.

José Simón Díaz, *Manual*, lists a total of thirty-nine of these collections published between 1609 and 1796.[6] Most of them are one-volume publications. They include not only *comedias* and *autos sacramentales* but also shorter farcical plays called *entremeses* ("interludes") and similar pieces.

However, there is one outstanding collection. Its title is *Comedias nuevas escogidas de los mejores ingenios de España* ("New plays selected from the best creative minds of Spain") and consists of forty-eight *partes* published between 1652 and 1704. It is usually cited in the abbreviated form *Comedias nuevas escogidas* or simply the *Escogidas Collection*. There is a considerable lapse of time between *Parte* XLVII (1681) and *Parte* XLVIII (1704). Volumes I-XLVII were published almost regularly, one each year, although there are gaps of several years between some volumes. However, more than one consecutive volume was published in some years, as many as four (XVI-XIX) in 1662. There is another earlier collection, known as *Comedias de diferentes autores* (1611-1652), which is bibliographically very complex.[7]

You may ask how bibliographical unity or consistency was

---

5. Edward M. Wilson and Duncan Moir, *The Golden Age: Drama 1492-1700* (London and New York, 1971), p. 91; part of *A Literary History of Spain*, ed. R. O. Jones, consisting of 8 volumes, not consecutively numbered.

6. José Simón Díaz, *Manual de Bibliografía de la literatura española*, 2nd edn. (Barcelona, 1966), pp. 115-16.

7. See La Barrera, pp. 683-7.

established over the decades. The significant part of the title page of *Parte* I reads: "*Primera parte de comedias escogidas de los mejores ingenios de España...* Madrid, por Domingo García y Morrás a costa de Juan de San Vicente, mercader de libros, 1652." This means that the bookseller Juan de San Vicente gave the order to print to the printshop of Domingo García y Morrás. The volumes are consecutively numbered with the title formula as introduced for *Parte* I appearing with some variations on the title page of almost all the volumes. However, publisher and printer change, but not the place of publication, which is always Madrid. The appearance of the volumes of the *Escogidas Collection* and the willingness of the publishers to invest can only mean that there had developed a substantial reading public for the plays of the *comedia*.

(3) *Suelta* **Editions.**

The trend of the reading public interested in the *comedia* continued through the eighteenth century. The demand was now primarily satisfied by *suelta* editions, which dominated the market. These editions are paperbound and consist on the average of sixteen folios, with or without a colophon indicating publisher, place, and year of publication.

From the outset one would assume that these editions, reprints of other texts closer to the original, are not of major value for the establishment of a reliable text. But no one knows for sure. At any rate every textual critic has to find out whether *suelta* editions exist and he has to evaluate them as to their importance for the history of the text on which he is working.

Twelve *suelta* editions sometimes were bound together and published with a title page, as another edition of an already existing *parte* in the collection of a single author or of a collection of various authors. These editions are easily distinguished from the genuine volume because they have no continuous foliation. Furthermore, private bibliophiles interested in the *comedia* assembled *sueltas* in bound volumes. In the University of Pennsylvania Rare Book Collection there are twenty-four such volumes collected by the Imperial Ambassador Count Bonaventura Harrach during his three assignments to the court in Madrid in

1664, 1673-76, and 1697-98.

B. Manuscripts

In principle, a manuscript text has neither more nor less authority than a printed text. There is, however, one obvious exception to this rule: the autograph or, strictly speaking, the holograph manuscript, written in its entirety by the playwright himself and signed by him. We are particularly fortunate in the case of Lope de Vega. Forty-three autograph manuscripts have survived, not all of them published in scholarly editions.[8] Also in respect to Lope de Vega, another exception has to be made. I am speaking of the so-called Gálvez manuscripts. Ignacio de Gálvez was an (or the) archivist in 1762 for the house of the Duke of Sessa, a descendant of the Duke of Sessa whose private secretary Lope de Vega was. The Duke was Lope's patron and the first collector of autograph manuscripts of his *comedias*. Gálvez copied thirty-two Lope plays with the date of composition in Lope's hand and his signature at the end. Gálvez is, on the whole, considered to have been a faithful copyist so that the Gálvez copies are of crucial importance for the chronology of Lope's plays and for establishing an authentic text. We will have to come back to the Gálvez manuscripts shortly.[9]

Just a brief word about Calderonian manuscripts. There are 418 dramatic manuscripts catalogued in Simón Díaz's *Bibliografía*.[10] Twenty-four of these are autographs, most of them autograph in their entirety, some of them only partially. Some are signed by Calderón. A few scholarly editions of Calderonian autograph manuscript *comedias* have recently appeared. Most of the autographs are kept in Madrid libraries. However, there must be more manuscripts of Calderón's *comedias* and *autos sacramentales* in existence. The Hispanic Society of America in New

8. See Walter Poesse, *The Internal Line-Structure of Thirty Autograph Plays of Lope de Vega* (Bloomington, 1949); a list of forty-two autographs is on pp.83-8, to which add *El primero Benavides* (1600).

9. See Augustín G. Amezúa, *Una colección manuscrita y desconocida de comedias de Lope de Vega Carpio* (Centro de Estudios sobre Lope de Vega, Cuaderno núm. 1; Madrid, 1945).

10. José Simón Díaz, *Bibliografía de las literaturas hispánicas*, VII (Madrid, 1967), pp. 63-96.

York has thirty-eight manuscripts, most of them *autos*. Three of originally five manuscripts were found in 1959 by Professor Václav Cerný in the library of Kuenburg Castle in Mladá Vožice in Czechoslovakia. One of these was a hitherto unknown play, *El gran Duque de Gandía*, published by Professor Cerný in 1963.

An autograph may be a fair copy or it may show corrections by the playwright himself and/or by others such as the theatrical producer. The playwright may have given the draft to a theatrical company or possibly in some cases to the bookseller. Furthermore, the autograph may not even be the most authentic last version of the play. The poet may have later modified his work to a greater or lesser degree, and the modifications could then appear in the printed text. Another note of caution concerning so-called autographs: proud nineteenth-century collectors were only too ready to declare their cherished possession an autograph. Actually, the determination of a manuscript as an autograph is possible only if it is signed by the author or if a sufficient number of genuine autographs are available with which to compare the manuscript in question.

C. Evaluation of the Textual Transmission, 1600-1800.

We have come to the end of our necessarily brief and selective bibliographical sketch. Now we shall consider the value of these publications in their reliability concerning the text and the problem of authorship.

Excluding for the moment those manuscripts which can be definitely established as genuine autographs, we must state that the texts have to be approached with the greatest caution, both as to their accuracy and as to authorship. Modern scholarship has made considerable contributions toward clarifying these problems, as we shall see later. But for the moment we shall consider the important preliminary question of how the plays reached the printer in the first place, and of the source of the manuscripts.

I am not aware of any comprehensive study of these problems. However, some piecemeal information is available. We know that Lope de Vega wrote his plays for the directors of theatrical companies, called *autores*, or for specific actors and actresses. We know, furthermore, that plays were traded among the directors of these companies. And the extant dramatic manuscripts often show visible traces of preparation of the plays for performance, with portions marked by *sí* or *no* in the margin of the page to indicate whether the passage so marked should be performed or omitted. But that still does not explain how the written texts got into print. In the case of some plays, we know that the theatres were what we would today call "bugged". There were a few people known as *grandes memorias* who sat through several performances and wrote down what they remembered. They were, of course, hired by the booksellers. These cases, however, must have been exceptional. Normally, more than one manuscript copy of any play must have existed within a company, for memorizing roles, for prompting, and for similar purposes, all copies ultimately deriving from the original, with or without textual changes wrought by the stage director. These copies must then have been sold to the bookseller. It is easy to see the number of errors which might occur during the manuscript's journey from the playwright through the performing companies to the printer.

As for the problem of authenticity of authorship, we have the complaints of the playwrights themselves. I have already mentioned Tirso de Molina's remarks in the Prologue of his *Segunda parte*. Lope de Vega claimed to have edited his plays himself from *Parte* IX to *Parte* XX because he was disgusted with the distortions his own texts had previously suffered. Lope's outbursts are numerous throughout his life.[11] One example must suffice. In the Prologue to *Parte* XVII (1621) Lope invents two lawsuits by the allegorical character *El Teatro* against the booksellers. The booksellers win each time because they prove that once the playwrights (*"los ingenios"*) are paid they no longer have any rights at all to their plays (*"no tenían acción sobre ellas"*). There exists complete chaos: the *autores* steal the plays from each other or they sell them to the towns which need them for their festivities. They insert other verses where it pleases them, or they steal or buy these from playwrights' secretaries (*"papelistas y secretarios cómicos"*). Lope ends by complaining that the most harmful thing

11. See Lope Félix de Vega Carpio, *La Dorotea*, ed. Edwin S. Morby (2nd edn., revised; Berkeley and Los Angeles, 1968), p. 54, n. 18.

for an author is to have his *comedias* printed. The poet cannot control the publication — especially when he never even kept a copy of his work.[12]

Calderón in *Parte* IV (Madrid, 1674) complains about the changes ("*yerros*") in his own plays but also about the publishing of others' plays under Calderón's name, and the cutting off of the end of an act or even of a play just to save paper.[13] Copyright protection was weak. The *privilegios* were granted only for ten years and were limited to a province. Therefore the booksellers could easily capitalize on famous names.

The booksellers claimed authenticity for their texts sometimes by calling their *partes* "*perfecta*" or "*verdadera*". On what basis they made these claims is not known. In some cases they advertised in their title pages "*sacadas de los originales*" ("taken from the originals"). But of what nature were the originals? The playwright's autograph manuscript or a copy directly derived from it? Probably not.

I realize that the information provided here is very spotty. What is needed at this time is a systematic collection of the facts so far known and a further search through title pages and the preliminary material of seventeenth-century collections.

There is, however, a deeper reason for authorship confusion. The *comedia* is the most powerful national theatre in existence, in that it expresses in dramatic-poetic form the ideals of the Spanish people of its time (i.e., of the first decades of the seventeenth century). And it was the genius of Lope de Vega — the genius of conformity — which had created the *comedia*'s structural formula, its thematology, and particularly its poetic language with its metaphors and imagery. Since "literature", that is, poetry, was in the air, Lope would be imitated, or, more accurately, Lope's formula could be used as a vehicle of expression by any fairly gifted writer. Thus it was really Lope himself who, in the last analysis, is the cause of the confusion. No wonder, then, that the problem of authorship plagues present-day scholarship. But may I add the somewhat heretical opinion that it is not so terribly important to

12. See Américo Castro and Hugo A. Rennert, *Vida de Lope de Vega (1562-1635)* (Salamanca, etc., 1968), p. 262.
13. Simón Díaz, *Bibliografía*, VII, p. 59.

attribute plays to specific authors. The *comedia* is a collective enterprise, which can be compared to Spanish balladry, the *Romancero*, the texts of which underwent many transformations in their transmission through space and time.[14]

II. Scholarship and Editorial Practices, 1800-1975.

The Romantic Period, as you all know, brought about a deep interest in the history and literature of nations, and not only of scholars' own nations but also of whole regions, as part of an all-embracing history of the humanities. The first histories of Spanish literature appeared in Germany (1804), in France (1813), and in North America and in England (1849). Friedrich Bouterweck in 1804 dedicated Volume II of his *Geschichte der neueren Poesie und Beredsamkeit* to Spain. It formed in itself part of his *Geschichte der Künste und Wissenschaften*. J. Ch. L. Simonde de Sismondi in 1813 wrote *De la littérature du midi de l'Europe*, of which Volumes III and IV deal with *Histoire de la littérature espagnole*. Finally, we have George Ticknor's *History of Spanish Literature* (New York and London, 1849) in three volumes. All three works were translated in due time into Spanish. The first history of Spanish literature written by a Spaniard is Antonio Gil de Zárate's *Resumen histórico de la literatura española* (Madrid, 1844).

The most urgent need, in satisfying the re-awakened interest in the study of literature, was to make the texts widely accessible. We shall restrict ourself to the theatre and proceed as far as possible in chronological order. The first attempt to create a collection of the Spanish theatre was made before the beginning of the nineteenth century. Vicente García de la Huerta, a successful dramatist in his own right, published *Theatro Hespañol* in sixteen volumes (Madrid, 1785-86). Despite the general title, the collection is limited to plays by Calderón and his contemporaries and to the editor's own plays. Much more ambitious was Eugenio de Ochoa. He edited *Colección de los mejores autores españoles* in sixty volumes (Paris, 1838-72). The first six volumes bear the title *Tesoro del teatro español desde su origen (año de 1356) hasta nuestros días; arreglado y dividido en cuatro partes por Eugenio de Ochoa* ("Treasures of the Spanish Theatre

14. Castro and Rennert, pp. 262-3.

from its origin (in the year 1356) until the present; arranged and divided into four parts by Eugenio de Ochoa") (Paris, 1838-40). For the first time the Spanish theatre is presented in chronological sequence: Vol. I, Theatre before Lope de Vega; II, Lope de Vega; III, Calderón; IV, Major Dramatists, contemporaries of Lope and Calderón; V, Other Dramatists of the second half of the seventeenth and eighteenth and early nineteenth centuries. Vol. VI (1840) is an anthology from the preceding five volumes. The scholarly intent of Ochoa's *Tesoro* is obvious from its organization.

From German romanticism and its preference for Calderón came the edition of his *comedias* by Juan Jorge Keil, in four volumes (Leipzig, 1827-30). In the title the editor claims that the texts were "*cotejadas* ["collated"] *con las mejores ediciones hasta ahora publicadas, corregidas y dadas a luz por....*" The sequence of 108 plays follows exactly the Vera Tassis edition. At the beginning of Volume IV we find plaintive observations about the unreliability of the texts due to the sloppiness and looseness of editorial policy of the printers and publishers. For a final fifth volume Keil promises to list variants in the most important editions, to offer notes explaining difficult passages and proper names, to indicate the sources of the plots and to speculate about the time of composition of the plays. Volume V unfortunately never appeared. We have to wait until 1890 when a comparable enterprise was undertaken by the Royal Spanish Academy in publishing the plays by Lope (see below).

The year 1846 is a milestone in the history of Spanish literature. In that year the enterprising printer Manuel Rivadeneyra (1805-72) published in Madrid the first volume of the fundamental collection *Biblioteca de Autores Españoles (BAE)*, which made easily accessible the texts of Spanish literature up to the early nineteenth century. By 1880, seventy-one volumes had appeared, including the Index. The *BAE* is now (from 1954) being reprinted and much enlarged; the last volume (CCLXVIII) on the shelves of the University of Pennsylvania Library is dated 1974. The *Comedia*, including the *autos sacramentales*, is represented in altogether sixteen volumes: Lope in four, Calderón in four, *Dramáticos contemporáneos a Lope de Vega* in two, etc. The editors Juan Eugenio Hartzenbusch (for Lope, Calderón, and Tirso de

Molina) and Ramón de Mesonero Romanos (for *Dramáticos contemporáneos*) were writers and critics rather than scholars. Hartzenbusch, like García de la Huerta before him, was a dramatist. Hartzenbusch was well aware of the wretched condition of his copy texts, and tried to correct some of the more obvious mistakes. Some other passages he "improved" as he saw fit. In addition, he divided the acts into scenes. But more accurate editions will appear in the future, he declares. The merit of having made available so many plays to the public far outweighs the unreliability of the texts, unavoidable at that time. Unfortunately, the faulty texts of the *BAE* volumes are still carried on in many modern uncritical commercial publications of *comedias*.

We encounter a scholarly edition of a collection for the first time in 1887. I am referring to the two volumes of *Ocho comedias desconocidas*, edited by Adolf Schaeffer.[15] Schaeffer is the author of the *Geschichte des spanischen Nationaldramas* (Leipzig, 1890), a work actually limited to the theatre of the Golden Age. The eight plays are reprinted from a volume of twelve, evidently a *parte*, the title and the usual preliminaries wanting, and consisting of 309 numbered leaves. Schaeffer successfully tries to determine the date of the volume, between 1612 and 1618, from the evidence available. As to the establishment of a reliable text, he complains about the impossibility *"de fijar un texto puro y exacto al mismo tiempo"* ("to establish a text which would be both pure and exact"), about misprints, and about looseness of plot structure and the syntax of the dramatists. He makes very few attempts at emendation and has practically no notes. His scholarship, then, is limited to determining the date of the volume. In addition, he briefly discusses each of the twelve plays, mostly from the bibliographical point of view.

We now proceed to consider the modern editions of Lope de Vega and of Calderón. But we have first to say a few words about the founder of modern scholarship and criticism of Spanish literature, Marcelino Menéndez Pelayo (1856-1912). His knowledge of the ancient classics and of Spanish literature of the late Middle

---

15. *Ocho comedias desconocidas de don Guillem de Castro, del Licenciado Damian Salustio del Poyo, de Luis Vélez de Guevara etc. tomadas de un libro antiguo de comedias, nuevamente hallado y dadas a luz por Adolf Schaeffer* (Leipzig, 1887), 2 vols.

Ages and the two centuries of the Golden Age was encyclopedic. It can truly be said that his achievements gave the initial impulse to the literary-historical studies in this area which are being carried on in Spain and abroad at the present time. The first part of his life was dedicated to the history of theology and of aesthetics, but later the direction of his investigations veered toward literary history. He published an *Antología de poetas líricos castellanos* (1890-1908) and *Orígenes de la novela* (1905-10). They contain both texts and very extensive historical and evaluative studies. And here is where the *comedia* comes in. In 1890 he began to edit the *Obras de Lope de Vega*, consisting of fifteen volumes by 1913, under the auspices of the Real Academia Española. This was a "monumental" edition in the literal sense of the word. The volumes are printed on heavy paper, and the texts are amply spaced, so that the Academy Edition looks more like a monument to the memory of Lope de Vega than a book that physically can be handled with ease. Menéndez Pelayo's introductions are still invaluable, primarily for his investigations into the sources of the plays at hand, supported by extensive excerpts from them. These sources included chronicles, Italian *novelle*, *romances* ("ballads") and so forth. Menéndez Pelayo's aesthetic judgment, his evaluation of the plays, is to be understood in the light of the prevailing standards of his time and of his personal preferences and prejudices. He was a classicist and an orthodox Catholic, but he was also an ardent Spaniard. I think that his deeprooted integration (like Lope's own) into what globally is termed *españolismo* ("Spanishness") is the reason for his finely tuned sensibility to the values of Lope's theatre, although this theatre is or at least seems to be running counter to the orderly structure of the classical play of antiquity.

Menéndez Pelayo expounded sound editorial principles in the *Observaciones generales* to his edition of Lope's plays. However, considering the magnitude of the project and the purpose of the Academy edition, he settles for the middle road between an edition destined for the general public ("*edición vulgar*") and a critical edition.[16] A collation of the autograph manuscripts of *Carlos V en Francia* and *El primero Benavides* shows

---

16. See Menéndez Pelayo, *Estudios sobre el teatro de Lope de Vega*, I (Santander, 1949), pp. 11-20. (Edición Nacional de las obras completas de Menéndez Pelayo, XXIX).

that in most cases the Academy edition follows the *parte* text; in these two instances, however, the autograph manuscripts were not available to Menéndez Pelayo.

After Menéndez Pelayo's death, the edition of Lope's plays was continued from 1916 to 1930, in the *Nueva edición de la Real Academia Española de las obras de Lope de Vega* under the general editorship of Emilio Cotarelo y Mori, with the plays edited by himself and others.

Nothing at all was done for Calderón at this time. Menéndez Pelayo, in his formative years, was not particularly attracted to him, and was even repulsed by Calderón's bloody honor plays, although he later changed his opinion. So his contribution to Calderón studies is limited to the collection of his lectures under the title *Calderón y su teatro. Conferencias*, published at the occasion of the bicentenary of Calderón's death in 1881.

Finally we come to the first critical edition of a *comedia*. The French Hispanist Alfred Morel-Fatio in 1877 edited the autograph manuscript of Calderón's *El mágico prodigioso* ("The Miracle-Working Magician"). This manuscript is the first draft of the play, but it is incomplete in the sense that Calderón did not write the conclusion, though the manuscript is of the quite unusual length of 3722 lines. In the Introduction Morel-Fatio discusses the sources of the play, offers a critical analysis, speaks about scene division in the *comedia*, and has observations about language and versification in *El mágico*. At the end he describes the manuscript and gives the bibliography of the subsequent printed editions and translations. The text is supported by a critical apparatus, consisting of the manuscript reading and its corrections put in by Calderón himself, and the collation with the *princeps* of 1663 and with *Parte* VI of the Vera Tassis edition of 1683 and the nineteenth-century editions by Keil and Hartzenbusch. The topics touched on in the Introduction and the variants noted at the foot of the page set a pattern which is still more or less followed today.

The next decade sees the remarkable editions by Max Krenkel of four Calderonian plays: *La vida es sueño* and *El príncipe constante* (1881); *El mágico prodigioso* (1885); *El alcalde* ["mayor"] *de Zalamea* (1887). His models were the German annotated editions of the ancient classics. All four editions have source studies which become more extensive, with ample excerpts, from edition to edition. The texts of *La vida* and *El príncipe* are based on Hartzenbusch, collated with Keil. For the text of *El mágico* Morel-Fatio's edition was a firm basis. The distinction of the *Alcalde* edition is that Krenkel was able to give not only Calderón's text but also that of the play of the same title attributed to Lope, from a rare *suelta*. The Calderonian *Alcalde* text is based on the *princeps*, a *suelta* of 1651, collated with Vera Tassis, *Parte* VII (1683), Keil, and Hartzenbusch. Krenkel is the first editor who supplies ample annotation to the text itself. His main procedure is to illuminate the text in hand with parallel passages from other plays, mostly but not exclusively Calderonian: which reveals his uncommonly wide reading (and an excellently organized card file). Furthermore, there are detailed grammatical and stylistic annotations in the manner found in commentaries on Latin and Greek texts.

Another twenty-five years go by until rigorous philological scholarship takes root in Spain under the leadership of Ramón Menéndez Pidal (1869-1968). He was primarily a medievalist and a linguist, but he also contributed to the study of the *comedia* by initiating the series of critical editions of autographs known as *Teatro Antiguo Español*, sponsored by the *Centro de Estudios Históricos* (founded in 1910). Menéndez Pidal opened the series himself in 1916 with the edition of *La serrana* ["mountain maid"] *de la Vera* by Luis Vélez de Guevara, prepared by him and his wife. Editions of nine plays have appeared, the last in 1940. These editions aim at a text established with the maximum precision the source material permits. The spelling of the autograph manuscript is exactly reproduced, "*pues sin este respeto fundamental no puede haber la exactitud necesaria para la crítica del texto*" ("because without this fundamental respect there cannot be the exactness indispensable to textual criticism").[17] Accentuation and punctuation are modernized. This is still the present-day practice. In the *Observaciones y notas* the editors study dramatic works with related themes. The practice has been followed by later editors, but I do not know whether in all those scholarly editions where such a study would have been possible. In the edition of Lope's *El primero*

17. See Luis Vélez de Guevara, *La serrana de la Vera*, eds. R. Menéndez Pidal and M. Goyri de Menéndez Pidal (Teatro Antiguo Español, I; Madrid, 1916), p. vii.

Benavides,[18] we followed the example set by William L. Fichter, editor of Lope's autograph manuscript of *El sembrar* ["sowing"] *en buena tierra* (New York, 1944).

There is one major achievement which remains to be mentioned: the successful search for objective criteria to establish authorship and at least an approximate date for the composition of a *comedia*. These criteria are two: (1) the study of the versification of an author; (2) an almost clinical observation of an author's orthöepy. The first study concentrating on Lope with emphasis on versification is by Milton A. Buchanan, *The Chronology of Lope de Vega's Plays* (Toronto, 1922). Buchanan studied Lope's preferences for nine metres in dated plays from 1593 to 1635 and in twelve plays by three other playwrights. He established the frequency of use of each metre in each play in terms of percentages. Thus the first play, *El favor agradecido* ("A favor gratefully received") of 1593, has 55% *redondillas*, 13% *quintillas*, and 5% *romance*, all native Spanish metres, and 22% Italianate verses, that is, eleven-syllable lines. In the last play of 1634, *Las bizarrías* ["gallantry"] *de Belisa*, there are only 22% *redondillas*, no *quintillas*, but 54% *romance* and 11% *décimas* (which appear only twice before ca. 1605-11). Buchanan illustrates orthöepy through the example of the word *diablo* which can be either a two-syllable or a three-syllable word. After a number of preliminary studies by S. Griswold Morley, which go back to 1905, of the versification of other playwrights, in 1940 the team of S. Griswold Morley and Courtney Bruerton published their monumental *The Chronology of Lope de Vega's Comedias* (New York). They succeeded in dating, at least within certain limited time spaces, 314 plays, and cautiously stated their opinion about 186 plays of doubtful or not certain authenticity which were printed under Lope's name. Their findings were confirmed through the above-mentioned Gálvez manuscripts. In seventeen cases checked the ratio between right and wrong was 82.35:17.65.[19]

Much of what is to be said about present-day practice is implicit in my survey of editorial techniques in the nineteenth and

18. Lope Félix de Vega Carpio, *El primero Benavides*, eds. Arnold G. Reichenberger and Augusta E. Foley (Philadelphia, 1973).
19. Amezúa, p. 22.

twentieth centuries. A great number of scholarly editions of single plays have appeared in the last half century, mostly in England, Canada, and the United States. This is not the place to give you a sort of spoken review article of recent editions. Instead, with due immodesty, I shall speak mainly about my own experiences. I have published one edition (Granada, 1956) based on printed texts, Luis Vélez de Guevara's *El embuste acreditado* ("The successful trick"), and two editions (Philadelphia, 1963 and 1973) based on autographs by Lope, *Carlos V en Francia* and *El primero Benavides*, the latter with Augusta E. Foley. I shall speak first about the editorial problems presented by the text, both printed and autograph. Next, I shall discuss the Introduction and finally the Notes.

Altogether sixteen editions are recorded for the Vélez play, either printed or manuscript, and under various titles and variously attributed to Luis Vélez de Guevara, his son Juan, Rey de Artieda, and Juan de Zabaleta. The text resulting from the collation of the nine available texts is based on the *princeps*, appearing in the *Quinta parte* (Madrid, 1653) of the *Escogidas Collection*, but incorporates the text published in *Parte treinta y cuatro* (Madrid, 1670) of the same collection under the title *El disparate creído* ("Crazy jokes believed") with Juan de Zabaleta as the author, and a manuscript with still another title, *Otro demonio tenemos* ("Another ghost we got"), by *tres ingenios*. Each edition has passages the other editions do not have. I decided to print everything I found: in other words, to create a composite text. Is this the original Vélez text? I doubt it. The corrections and modifications by stage directors or censors, changes by printers, and a possible *refundición* ("adaptation") by Zabaleta are included in the text. We have, in short, a classic example of how a play, under the prevailing circumstances, became public property.

The text is reproduced with spelling, accents, and punctuation modernized except when the ancient orthography reflects actual pronunciation; strophic division is marked by indentation. The verses are numbered and the corresponding pages or folios are indicated in the margins. If a verse is shared by two or, as sometimes in Calderón, by three speakers, each fraction of the verse goes into a new line, not flush with the beginning of the verse but moved one space to the right of where the first part of the verse ends in the preceding line. The variant readings are listed at the foot of the page.

Considering the bibliographical conditions of the *comedia*, of which the Vélez text is a typical example, it will not surprise anyone that no critical edition of the total work of any playwright has been attempted. Only in the case of Calderón have preliminary bibliographical studies been undertaken, mainly by H. C. Heaton and his pupil Everett W. Hesse in the 1940s and by Edward M. Wilson and his pupil Don W. Cruickshank since 1959.[20] In 1973 D. W. Cruickshank and J. E. Varey published "reliable [facsimile] reprints of the first editions of all nine *partes de comedias* [by Calderón] and, in the case of the first five *partes*, of the reprints which appeared during his lifetime."[21] In nineteen volumes they "[makc] available ... the material necessary for a textual study of all those works which appeared in the collective volumes of his plays in the course of the seventeenth century."[21] This edition means a most significant new beginning of serious textual criticism, not only for Calderón, but for all dramatists.

Professor Hans Flaschc, University of Hamburg, is circulating libraries in Spain to obtain information about their holdings of Calderonian manuscripts. He aims at producing a critical edition of the *autos*, hopefully for 1981, the tercentenary of Calderón's death. In addition, between 1962-63 and 1975 he has published a critical edition of Calderón's *auto sacramental La vida es sueño* (which is the religious version of the play) in five installments which he calls "*Bausteine* ["building blocks"] *zu einer kritischen und kommentierten Ausgabe Calderóns.*"[22]

The editorial problems presented by the autograph manuscripts are relatively simple. Assuming that the autograph is the final form of the play, we have the authoritative text before us. Thus the editor's task is to read or sometimes to decipher the manuscript. In the case of the two Lope plays reading and tran-

20. See Wilson and Moir, pp. 160-1.

21. Pedro Calderón de la Barca, *Comedias*, facsimile edition, 19 vols. eds. D. W. Cruickshank and John Varey (London, 1973), I, vii.

22. Hans Flasche, "Bausteine zu einer kritischen und kommentierten Ausgabe Calderóns," no. 1, "Beitrag zu einer kritischen und kommentierten Ausgabe des Auto sacramental 'La vida es sueño' von Calderón," in *Homenaje a Johannes Vincke*, II (Madrid, 1962-63). The other four *Beiträge* appear in *Gesammelte Aufsätze zur Kulturgeschichte Spaniens*, XXI (1963), XXII (1965), XXV (1970), and XXVIII (1975).

scribing the text was a relatively easy task, since Lope's handwriting, even when he writes in haste, is quite legible. And the presentation of the text on the printed page is not different from that of the text derived from printed editions, with the fundamental exception, of course, of respecting the spelling of the autograph. However, the exciting part of editing an autograph manuscript I have not mentioned yet: deciphering the corrections in Lope's own hand, that is, trying to read or to make out the deleted words. Lope himself always tried to make the discarded version more or less illegible, either by a series of loops or — less frequently — by veritable spots. It probably would provide a valuable insight into Lope's writing process to classify the changes as far as possible.

The critical apparatus is arranged below the text on two levels: first a detailed description of the text, analyzing the writing process which led to changes in the text, indicating how passages were marked for omission, and noting minor details. The second level lists the variants in selected printed texts. The autograph of *El primero Benavides* contains 163 lines more than the *princeps* (Madrid, 1609). Since we are fortunate to have the original, we found it unnecessary to collate the text as it appears in the other seven located editions of the *Segunda parte*. Nor have we consulted a manuscript copy in an eighteenth-century hand preserved in the Library of the University of Seville. The variants listed are limited to those of the *princeps* and the two modern editions most currently in use, the Academy edition and the selection of Lope plays published by Aguilar (Madrid, 1955).

The Introduction ought to study the play as a whole and ought to deal with the following matters: bibliography, date of composition, structural analysis and versification, sources, and final evaluation. I already have discussed bibliography in my remarks on the editor and his text. The date of composition is given on the autographs themselves: for *El primero Benavides*, "*En Madrid a 15 de junio de 1600, Lope de Vega Carpio;*" for *Carlos V en Francia*, "*En Toledo, a 20 de noviembre de 1604, Lope de Vega Carpio.*" The first edition of *El embuste* appeared in 1653, nine years after Vélez' death. I arrived at the date of 1617-18 by circumstantial evidence: (a) certain contacts with the works by Cervantes published in 1615, (b) similarities to other Vélez plays of the same period, and (c) the versification of *El embuste* compared with that of plays by Lope and Guillén de Castro composed between 1615 and 1620. Next, the editor should not simply retell the plot but should provide a structural analysis of the play, guided by changing verse forms. In 1609 Lope made some sweeping statements about the employ of the most frequent metres, statements which, although confirmed by modern editors and students, do not cover the metres' entire functional range. In general one can only say that a change of metre, most of the time but certainly not always, indicates a change in mood and atmosphere. In many editions, however, the analysis of versification is no more than a routine appendix of the Introduction. As for sources, the search clearly varies from play to play. In *El embuste* there are some episodes definitely borrowed from Cervantes, but beyond that there are no specific "sources". There are only motives. The principal motive is magic as practised by the servant Merlín, the main mover of the action. The theme of the play is the conflict between love and honor, certainly a most traditional and conventional theme in the *comedia*. But it is treated almost farcically. In *Carlos V en Francia* there are historical works which Lope demonstrably used. I had to reconstruct for Act I the historical background of the meeting in Nice in 1538 between the archrivals Charles V and Francis I of France, with Pope Paul III as the intermediary; the political events of the Cortes of Toledo of 1538 for Act II; and the splendid ceremonial entry of the Emperor into Paris in 1540 for Act III. In *El primero Benavides* we had to investigate the history of the kingdom of León around the year 1000. We tried to answer the question of what motivated Lope to write a genealogical play in 1600 about the origin of the Benavides family. We did not find any specific answer beyond the general observation that Lope wrote other genealogical plays with the action taking place at the beginning of Spanish history, an age of military prowess in the struggle against the Moors, with violent power struggles among the leading nobles on the one hand, and rural simplicity and monarchical devotion on the other hand. Lope glorified the heroic age of Spanish history. He emerged as a relatively faithful recorder of history in both plays: always, of course, as the dramatic poet he was, subordinating historical facts to his dramatic and patriotic art. Thus in *El primero Benavides* he placed the action of the play at the time of the boy king Alfonso V, crowned in 999, whose life is saved by the protagonist Sancho, the first Benavides. Actually, the "first Benavides" would have lived during the reign of Alfonso VII, Emperor of Castile and León (1105-50).

I am quite aware of the fact that source study *per se* is not literary criticism. But the relationship between the raw material of the sources and the finished work is an important contribution to that fundamental question of our profession: how reality is transformed into art.

Finally, a word about aesthetic evaluation, answering the question, "Is the play good, bad or indifferent?" and "Why is it as it is?" Value judgment is a problem. If we ask questions about plot development from scene to scene, or from act to act, or about the motivation provided for the characters, we bring analytical points of view to bear on the play which we (or my generation at least) have been taught to ask in high school. These are useful and practical questions and may reveal the true nature of the play. In the case of *Carlos V* it turns out that the play is episodic, each act having its own story and existence. Unity is provided by the protagonist, who appears in all three acts. As for characterization: Carlos V is all imperial dignity and is endowed with a steadfast moral fibre resisting sexual temptation. Pacheco is of the *miles gloriosus* type. Fernandillo is a girl disguised as a man in pursuit of her lover who refuses to marry her. The Emperor, upholding the laws of the land, sees to it that the lover does marry her. She is also a type: *la mujer vestida de hombre* ("woman dressed as a man"). The most interesting and original character is Leonor, *dama*, who is really a mental case. She is obsessed by love for Charles V and offers herself to him body and soul. Each of these characters pursues his or her goal so that several strains of subplot are winding their way through this *comedia*. Is it a good play? I do not know, but I think I understand it, and I like it.

The content and the extent of the Notes is a matter for the editor to decide. As a rule of thumb one might say that whatever the trained editor does not understand, or does not know, needs explanation, be it a name (mythological or historical, or a place name), a word not in use today in modern Spanish, a very specialized term of a craft, or of a piece of clothing, etc., a grammatical or morphological phenomenon different from what is found in modern Spanish, a complex syntactical construction, or some rhetorical device such as anaphora, alliteration, and chiasmus. The explanation and clarification of imagery and its symbolism, if any, is an open field. How much the editor should provide depends very much on his own response to it, that is, on his own knowledge and sensitivity. However, in annotating we have to avoid the pitfalls of overdoing it and of pedantry.

In our two countries, a model of editing and annotation was created by the late professors John M. Hill and Mabel Margaret Harlan in their volume *Cuatro Comedias* (New York, 1941), editing one play each of the four prominent dramatists, Lope, Alarcón, Tirso de Molina, and Calderón. This is the text through which I learned the ropes. To their memory and that of their pupil, my teacher Claude E. Anibal, I dedicate this contribution.

EDITING TEXTS IN MULTIPLE VERSIONS

William F. Hunter

I

The concepts and methods of textual criticism we are mainly concerned with here, the so-called genealogical or stemmatic principles, were developed over the last 150 years for dealing with Greek and Latin classical texts and the Greek text of the New Testament.[1] Many expositions of the basic terminology and concepts are available.[2] The validity and the practical value of the

1. For a historical outline of textual criticism see S. Timpanaro, *La genesi del metodo del Lachmann* (Florence, 1963); Bruce M. Metzger, *The Text of the New Testament. Its Transmission, Corruption, and Restoration*, second edition (Oxford, 1968), particularly pp. 149-85; or briefly, the excellent article 'Textual Criticism' by Edward John Kenney in *Encyclopaedia Britannica*, fifteenth edition (1977).

2. For example, Paul Maas, *Textkritik*, fourth edition (Leipzig, 1960), English translation (of an earlier edition) by Barbara Flower, *Textual Criticism* (Oxford, 1958); the article by Kenney cited above in note 1, and its predecessor by Fredson Bowers and the Editors in *Encyclopaedia Britannica* (1969); A. H. McDonald, the article 'Textual Criticism' in *Oxford Classical Dictionary*, second edition (Oxford, 1970); and my own earlier attempt at encouraging Calderonian editors to use stemmatic methods, 'Métodos de crítica textual', in *Hacia Calderón. Coloquio anglogermano Exeter 1969*, edited by Hans Flasche (Berlin, 1970), pp. 13-28.

methodology have been discussed, questioned, defended, elaborated, and adapted in numerous books and articles.[3] Examples of the proliferation of alternative or supplementary procedures can be examined in the critical editions, especially of classical, patristic, and medieval texts, on the shelves of any reasonable academic library. The prospective editor of Spanish Golden-Age dramatic texts, however, need not be dismayed in face of such a mountain of literature on methodology and the radical disagreements of theoreticians and practitioners. The potential problems are limited and simplified by both the character of our basic material (the texts and versions) and the nature and mode of application of the methods of textual criticism I shall outline.

In the first place, a comparatively small number of Spanish Golden-Age dramatic texts, or parts of them, are found in three or more extant independent versions (that is, MS or printed versions that are not directly descended from any other extant version), the normal minimum requirement for possible application of stemmatic recension.[4] And only in quite exceptional cases does the number of independent versions even approach double figures.[5] Printed editions stifled the production of MS copies for the interested public and led to the loss of those that we can assume, and sometimes prove, to have been produced up to the time of the printed edition; as a consequence, the earlier in the Golden-Age

3. Bibliography can be found in Timpanaro, Metzger, and Kenney, cited in note 1; D'Arco Silvio Avalle, 'La critica testuale', in *Grundriss der Romanischen Literaturen des Mittelalters* (Heidelberg, 1972-), I, 538-58, with bibliography at pp. 691-92; Jean Duplacy and Eric Huret, 'Classification des états d'un texte, mathématiques et informatique: repères historiques et recherches méthodologiques', *Revue d'Histoire des Textes*, 5 (1975), 249-309 (pp. 298-309). Elaborations and developments include Sir W. W. Greg, *The Calculus of Variants: an Essay on Textual Criticism* (Oxford, 1927), the work to which I owe most myself, and Vinton A. Dearing, *A Manual of Textual Analysis* (Berkeley and Los Angeles, 1959). A notable and influential critique of the genealogical method, with other valuable observations on editorial practice, will be found in *Piers Plowman: the A Version*, edited by George Kane (London, 1960); see further *Piers Plowman: the B Version*, edited by George Kane and E. Talbot Donaldson (London, 1975).

4. Occasionally, where contamination or conflation can be identified, or where there is some other source of information, the editor who has only two extant versions of his text may be able to deduce features of a lost independent version. Such a version, like the inferential versions we will discuss later, will take its place in the stemma that portrays all that can be discovered about the history of the transmission of the text. But it will help in establishing the final text only in respect of those features that can be recovered.

5. See, for example, Calderón's *El pleito matrimonial del Cuerpo y el Alma*, in the edition by Manfred Engelbert (Hamburg, 1969).

period a text is printed, normally the fewer the MSS now extant. Time itself and changes in literary taste and fashion have also played their part in the disappearance of MSS. Successive printed editions frequently, although not invariably, copied the one immediately preceding, and so do not provide independent versions.[6] Of the vast quantity of dramatic works which were not published, few seem to have been of sufficient value or interest to people outside the theatre for copies to be made or survive. Hardly any of the prompt-copies or actors' parts needed by the *autores* have survived, and the collections of scripts gathered by *cofradías*, town councils, and other authorities involved in the regulation, sponsoring, and presentation of religious and secular drama have also largely disappeared. The principal exceptions are the multiple MS copies of those of Calderón's *autos* unavailable in print until the posthumous Pando edition.

Furthermore, compared with, for example, classical or medieval texts, the textual transmission of Golden-Age dramatic texts is generally uncomplicated. However corrupt and doubtful the texts may be for other reasons, the stemmatic relations of the versions are usually simple. Contamination is rare and full conflation even rarer. There are many reasons for this. First, the vital period of textual history, the period of composition, copying, and recopying that produced the versions now extant which preserve significant information about the original version or versions, is short. Only in the case of some of Calderón's *autos* is it as long as 100 years; generally it is much less, depending on how long interest in the work lasted in the theatre or outside, including revivals, and on when a printed edition appeared that became the accepted basic text. The Calderonian period is prolonged by the posthumous resurgence of interest in his works. In the case of

6. Such copies, like non-independent MS copies, still have importance: first, as part of the history of publication of the text; second, as a record of the text readers at a certain time may have been using; third, as having potentially (though not always in fact) information in their punctuation, tell-tale readings, etc., about how the text was understood by those responsible for it in this form; fourth, where a copy differs from its copy-text, as showing the kind of error to which a particular passage is prone; fifth, as showing contemporary emendation of the text. When the copy-text is an extant printed version bibliographers can use non-independent printed versions to identify compositorial characteristics, printer's house style, etc., a knowledge of which may enable the textual critic to refine the evidence that the independent printed edition gives of its lost copy-text.

other authors too we may assume that the production of copies of their works was greater at some moments than at others, whatever the time-scale of the dynamic period. The likely number of MS copies of a play made during the period of active transmission is impossible to discover: they could include single MSS for theatrical, proprietorial, or administrative purposes, or for devotees, copies of their parts for actors, MSS in quantity for booksellers. There is less doubt about numbers of printed editions, since representatives are more likely to survive. But even where the total number of acts of copying may have been large, the number of master-copies is not, so that extant versions derive from a limited number of copy-texts. The shortness and coherence of dramatic texts also favour the integrity (as distinct from the quality) of versions during transmission, as does their character as light literature: being texts of little moment, true editorial activity, comparing versions as a means of castigating the text, does not really affect Golden-Age drama until the monumental collections of Calderón prepared by Vera Tassis and Pando or his editor, although there are earlier instances.

An editor must always be ready for the unexpected and the awkward, and he may well meet exceptions to the generalizations just stated on the basis of the small proportion of Golden-Age dramatic texts that have so far been adequately studied. But there is no need to prepare a general methodology that will take account of situations that may seldom or never arise. Provided the procedures will themselves reveal and not disguise anomalies and complications, they should be the simplest that will meet anticipated requirements. And being simple, and indeed mostly clarified common sense, they need little theoretical validation. The basic concepts and principles do, however, need to be clearly understood, because some easily made false assumptions lead to traps and pitfalls. Note too that the codifying and systematizing of the procedures contribute greatly to their efficiency. In favourable circumstances, and if applied conscientiously, such procedures will help in organizing and analysing the textual materials, clarify the history of the transmission of the text, and enable the editor to extract the maximum amount of relevant information. They will also be, to a certain degree at least, self-regulating, showing up anomalies or gaps that call for double checking, and at the same time provide an objective framework within which editorial speculation may more safely take place. Finally, it is important to note that the techniques of analysis of variants and stemmatic recension are not a closed and self-sufficient system of textual criticism. They themselves depend on all the other numerous skills and areas of expertise that editors have to acquire — in paleography, bibliography, philology, stylistics, human psychology, history, etc. — and they work in conjunction with the other sources of information and editorial techniques that lead to the establishing of a critical text. The wider the range of skills and areas of knowledge the editor has, the less likely he will be to miss anything of interest or importance, and the better in every respect will be his final text.

II

What, then, are the editor's general aims and prospects of success as he examines several divergent versions of a text, none of which has self-evident exclusive authority? The first task, and one that has its own importance for literary history, is to uncover and document the textual history of the work as a whole and of its constituent elements. The editor as textual critic analyses the relationships of the extant versions, draws stemmata, and determines the originality of readings or their probability of being original; he will also further note discernible corruptions that affect all extant versions and, if he can, suggest emendations of transmitted readings. The results of this primary study of the versions of the text are then used to prepare a version that approximates as closely as circumstances allow to what we infer is the author's original version or versions. (The notion of 'original version' is a simplification that we will subsequently have to qualify in different ways. See especially note 15.) Notice that the intention is not to determine which single extant copy is the most authoritative (although the fact that there is such a copy may emerge, and will be of great value), but to exploit the information in *all* the extant versions that will help towards recovering or reconstructing the lost authorial original, or, as is more likely, the earliest ancestor common to all the extant versions. The editor also, of course, normally functions as more than a textual critic.[7] He attends to the presentation of his text for the public, deciding (often under strict constraints laid on him by a publisher) format, lay-out, amount of textual information to be published, explanatory and interpretative annotation, and so on. And as part of this branch of his activity he may choose to go beyond the recovery of the authorial original and seek to correct obvious errors or defects attributable to the author that we may assume the author himself would have corrected had they been brought to his attention.[8] Whether or not to produce such an ideal or perfected text is a matter of policy that does not lie in the field of textual criticism; it belongs with such decisions as whether the final edition will take the form of a strict copy of one extant version (the *princeps*, say, or other version of special interest or worth) with emendations in footnotes, or will be an editorial version with the emendations incorporated, and whether the edition will be old-spelling or modernized.[9]

But if we can be clear about the general aims of textual criticism, we cannot be sanguine about the completeness and reliability of the final text that is produced. One only has to look at the state of some of the extant holograph foul papers, and to compare the texts of holographs with other MS or printed versions, or even compare different versions of works for which no authoritative copy is extant, to realize the possible corruption that may lie undetected and undetectable in many of our dramatic

---

7. Not all those who may legitimately be called editors are, or need to be, themselves textual critics. The type of editor meant here will be obvious from the context. The usurpation of the title by imposters and plagiarizers is a different matter.

8. Obviously the editor needs a suitably authoritative copy to be able to tell authorial errors from errors of transmission.

9. For some discussion of these and other points in relation to Spanish Golden-Age drama see Manfred Engelbert, 'Wie ediert man Dramen? Zur Problematik der Texte spanischer Klassiker', in *Texte und Varianten. Probleme ihrer Edition und Interpretation*, edited by Gunter Martens and Hans Zeller (Munich, 1971), pp. 355-69, although Engelbert makes some erroneous assertions about the circumstances in which copies of texts were made and published; my review of the edition of Calderón's *La cena del rey Baltasar* by Gerd Hofmann (Berlin and New York, 1971), in *BHS*, 51 (1974), 294-96; also *Play-texts in Old Spelling: Papers from the Glendon Conference*, edited by Raymond C. Shady and G. B. Shand (New York, 1983).

texts.[10] Dramatic authors, often writing at speed and to a deadline, produced foul papers full of illegibilities, deletions, and alterations. Sometimes they themselves made fair copies (some have survived — with their share of copying errors); in other cases the foul papers were passed to a commissioned copyist or to the *autor* for copying. At some point a legible and ostensibly final copy had to be prepared for submission to the censors for authorization of performance or publication. The possibilities of corruption at this earliest stage of transmission are at least as high as in later stages, and probably even higher. The master-copy or archetype of all subsequent versions, the only text we have any chance of recovering, may itself be sadly removed from what the author himself intended his text to be. Thereafter texts may suffer at the hands of naive and unlettered theatrical copyists, and occasionally of *memoriones*, whose expertise (if that is the proper word) was the memorizing of dramatic works as they were being performed so that unauthorized copies could be made.[11] Examples such as Calderón's *En la vida* (see note 10) show how in transmission the rare and the original are eliminated or conventionalized, jokes and puns vanish, learned or unfamiliar references are distorted. Later attempts at restoration of such corruptions may correct part of the error and at the same time damage good text around it. Theatrical texts are also liable to be cut and adapted before and during performance, whether or not the author approves, and again when revived. Being in verse too has its risks. Single lines, and more often pairs and groups of line, can easily be dropped in error; they can also be deliberately cut, as by printers of *sueltas* or cheap editions trying to make plays fit their format as economically as

10. All editors, as part of their basic preparation for their task, need to familiarize themselves with the forms in which texts were produced and circulated, in order to be alert to what may go wrong in transmission, and perhaps recognize and repair defects. For a particularly instructive comparison of an autograph MS with the subsequent versions see the edition of Calderón's *En la vida todo es verdad y todo mentira* by Don William Cruickshank (London, 1971). See also comments on the copy-text underlying printed editions of seventeenth-century English dramatic texts by G. R. Proudfoot, 'Dramatic Manuscripts and the Editor', in *Editing Renaissance Dramatic Texts English, Italian, and Spanish. Papers Given at the Eleventh Annual Conference on Editorial Problems, University of Toronto, 31 October — 1 November 1975*, edited by Anne Lancashire (New York and London, 1976), pp. 9-38.

11. For an example see José M. Ruano de la Haza, 'An Early Rehash of Lope's *Peribáñez*', *BCom*, 35 (1983), 6-29.

possible.[12] On the other hand, errors in scansion and rhyme are noticeable, and spontaneous and unauthentic repairs may be made. Short speeches in sections of rapid dialogue can easily be jumped by a copyist since the speaker's name is being frequently repeated. In MSS the location of speakers' names and especially of stage-directions in the margin opposite the appropriate part of the text is only approximate, and they can easily float to the wrong place. One could go on listing major factors likely to cause deterioration of dramatic texts in transmission, beyond the inevitable copyists' errors.[13] Little wonder that dramatists so often complained of the deplorable and even unrecognizable state of the texts of their plays that circulated and reached publication. Obviously not all non-holograph texts are equally corrupt; some have been well copied, some have been checked (more or less) or even revised by the author; Calderón's *autos* seem to have suffered much less than his plays; and of course it is still true that we can expect far more of a text to be transmitted accurately than inaccurately. But unless we have particular reasons for confidence, our claims for our texts should be modest and realistic.

III

As we have already noted, the editor will use every means and method open to him in examining and assessing his particular textual materials. But as complete a stemmatic map of the versions as can be arrived at is fundamental. In the first place, the variant readings and all peculiarities of relationship between the extant versions of the text have arisen in the course of the transmission

12. For some idea of the possible extent of loss through cutting see S. Griswold Morley and Courtney Bruerton, *The Chronology of Lope de Vega's 'Comedias'* (New York and London, 1940), particularly pp. 7-11, and the appendix to the revised Spanish edition, *Cronología de las comedias de Lope de Vega* (Madrid, 1968); John B. Wooldridge, 'Some Unstudied Aspects of Calderón's Versification', in *Critical Perspectives on Calderón de la Barca*, edited by Frederick A. de Armas, David M. Gitlitz, and José A. Madrigal (Lincoln, Nebraska, 1981), pp. 161-83 (pp. 167-68).

13. I need hardly stress the importance of getting to know the common types and sources of copying errors, not forgetting the important influence of house style in printed texts. The wider and more detailed the editor's knowledge of what could and did happen to texts in MSS or during printing, the greater will be his repertoire of strategies for analysing variants and perhaps repairing damage. See also above, note 10. Some examples of cuts and their different causes are examined in Margaret Rich Greer, 'Calderón, Copyists, and the Problem of Endings', *BCom*, 36 (1984), 71-81.

of the versions. Therefore only by reconstructing the history of the versions can we understand the history and even the nature of individual variants, especially where there is coincidence in error, progressive variation, correction, and conflation. And where we are left with gaps and doubts in the relationship of the extant versions and their readings, all speculation must take place within the limits of what we do know about the stemmatic relationships. In the second place, without a stemma there can be no stemmatic recension with the great benefits that derive from it.

In preparing an edition from multiple extant versions the editor is working at first in the dark and trying to trace his way backwards along the lines of transmission in order to recover versions of the text now lost that will bring him nearer to the author's original (or the earliest traceable version), but it will help explain some of the basic notions on which stemmatic recension depends, and also show some of the pitfalls, if we first examine simple models of straightforward transmission and genetic relationships with all the parts open to inspection. Actual case histories will not necessarily be as simple as the models: all sorts of defects and complications in the textual materials may make it difficult or even impossible fully to disentangle the stemmatic relationships and successfully apply stemmatic procedures for establishing the text. But these peculiarities in patterns of transmission are recognized and defined by reference to the normal modes.

It may be worth pointing out that, in the general statements that follow, 'text' can apply to a whole work or to any separate coherent part of it for which a fragmentary copy may exist, and the types of normal or straightforward relationship exemplified can apply to a whole stemma or to analogous patterns in any complete segment of a stemma. Some of my terminology could at times be misleading. It does not always match that of other writers, which probably does not matter greatly. Potentially more confusing, however, is the use of words such as 'version' and 'copy' in quite different senses at different times. Sometimes this is unavoidable, English language and usage being what they are. Sometimes, perhaps, more satisfactory terms might be found to keep the necessary distinctions, but I have failed to think of them. I can only hope that where the meaning is not self-evident I have given the necessary explanation. The validity of the concepts does not, of course, depend on the terminology. Fuller discussions of some of the terms have been placed at the end of this section (pages 39-44) to avoid complicating the simple demonstration.

The first empirically derived axiom of textual criticism is that, when a new manual copy of a text is made, variants appear, and so one copy can be distinguished from another.[14] The second axiom is that the bulk of a copytext is transmitted unchanged, and so copies retain features of all their ancestors.

Stemma 1

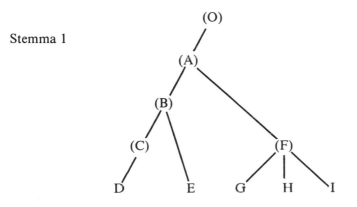

O is the author's original;
versions in parentheses are no longer extant.

Thus in Stemma 1, taking the successive copies from O to D, the bulk of the variants of A will pass to B (even in the most straightforward transmission we cannot expect all A's variants to be transmitted), and each further stage of transmission will add its variants to the accumulation of unoriginal readings that is transmitted to the final copy D along with original text. E will have, along with original text, variants that originated in A and B, and

14. The axiom may fail in very short texts or where exceptional vigilance coincides with good fortune. Although the physical entities can be differentiated, textually such identical witnesses are in effect one and the same, just as identical copies of a printed book. The phrase 'manual copy' is used to exclude reproduction of an original by, for example, photography and the multiple impressions of a printed text, where, barring accident or intervention, the original text is exactly duplicated.

also its own variants, but not variants that originated in C and D (although even in straightforward transmission there may be chance coincidence between variants in E and in C or D). G, H, and I will all share distinctive text derived from F (original text with variants from A, B, and F), but, like all extant independent versions, will be distinguished from each other by variants peculiar to themselves. See further the note on *Independent versions* on pages 43-44.

Some obvious facts and principles can be illustrated from the sample stemma — obvious when we have the whole story available to us, but sometimes forgotten when the editor has only extant versions and is working to construct a stemma. If D were the sole extant version, we could not tell which readings derived from O and which were variants, or at what point individual variants first appeared; we could not even know how many intermediate copies there were. For textual purposes these undiscoverable intermediate versions, known as *potential versions*, have to be ignored. If we emend obvious errors in our sole version D, we cannot be sure we have got closer to the original reading, since we may simply be returning to previously corrupted text. A text with no obvious defects is not necessarily authentic. Two considerations help prevent the defeatism that seems bound to strike the editor in such a situation. First, we know from the comparison of extant holograph MSS with other non-authorial versions that a fair proportion of any text will be transmitted faithfully from the author's original, even if we cannot now tell which parts of the extant version are authentic and which not. Second, the conquest of the authentic text is not the only valid exercise in literary history. While we always like to know 'what the author wrote and meant', in a historical perspective the public life of the work after it leaves the privacy of the author's desk is just as important, and even more so; and the extant version is the work as known to at least part of its public (compare note 6).

If we add a second extant independent version E, deriving from B, the situation is improved, but not greatly. When D and E agree, it will be because B's reading has passed to both, and the agreement of D and E confirms the reading. But whether B's reading was itself original or a variant introduced in A or B, we cannot know. When therefore we have two independent versions of a text agreeing, the earliest text we can hope to recover directly, using only preserved readings without emendation, are the readings of the most immediate common ancestor, that is, the version from which the lines of transmission diverge, B and not A in our example. We must not assume without reason that that common ancestor is O. If, on the other hand, our two versions D and E disagree, we cannot tell where either reading originated, whether in O, or in D or E themselves, or in any lost intermediate copy. We are thrown back on our personal judgment in choosing which reading to accept. And as we have seen, we may not be choosing between an original reading and a variant, but between two variants. The same holds true when, instead of two extant copies, we have two branches of the stemma witnessing to two lineal versions, whatever the number of extant copies. (For 'lineal versions', see in the note on *Version*, pages 42-43.)

When three or more independent versions are involved, the situation may be more complex. The simplest relationship is that of D, E, and F in Stemma 1. These are related solely through B. Where any two of the versions agree, we can be almost certain that the reading derives from B. If, however, our extant versions were D, E, G, H, and I in Stemma 1, we might find for particular readings the group GHI opposed to the group DE. This would not mean that the odds were three to two in favour of the reading in G, H, and I, since these have in F an *exclusive common ancestor*, an ancestor shared with no other extant version, and their agreement comes from that relationship. G, H, and I are witnesses to the single lineal version deriving from F. And F is the version to be compared with D and E in seeking to confirm the text of B, the exclusive common ancestor of these three versions. From this illustration, therefore, some further general principles can be drawn. When there are opposed readings, mere superiority in the number of versions is no guarantee of authenticity. We need to identify all the separate groups of versions that have exclusive common ancestors and use the readings of these groups to identify the text of lost ancestors, the *inferential versions*. Then we can work our way backwards along the lines of the stemma, comparing lineal versions at each stage. Whenever two or more of the versions that diverge at a particular node agree in their readings, we can infer that the readings came from their exclusive common ancestor.

When we have three or more extant versions, therefore, the fundamental step in establishing a stemma is identifying which groups have exclusive common ancestors. This is not simply a matter of noting which versions share the same readings. In Stemma 1, on a significant number of occasions, we would find the extant versions grouped against each other DE : GHI. But the same grouping would be produced by, for example, Stemma 2, where only the group DE has an exclusive common ancestor, or by Stemma 3, where the group DE and the group

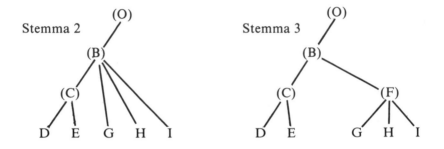

GHI both have exclusive common ancestors. Or again, in Stemma 1, when all the extant versions except D share a reading, it does not mean that EGHI have an exclusive common ancestor, as it would if the versions were related as in Stemma 4. What makes true *genetic groups* is not the sharing of readings,

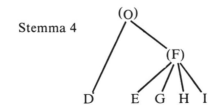

but the sharing of altered readings, that is, of readings which differ from the original or from some ancestor. Genetically distinct branches of the textual family carry altered readings derived from their exclusive common ancestor, as occurred in Stemma 1 with alterations in F, in Stemma 2 with alterations in C, and in Stemma 3 with alterations in some readings in C and in other readings in F. The vital factor therefore in classifying versions in genetic groups is the *direction of variation*.

How can we identify the direction of variation? If variants are regarded as neutral units, it will normally be impossible. An element of analysis is required. The analysis may use any of a whole range of considerations: grammatical, semantic, stylistic, orthographical, bibliographical, historical, etc., that show one reading as being earlier than another. Sometimes a single reading will have two or more variants in different versions that show clearly a progressive alteration of the text. In the initial stages of drawing up a stemma, such evidence by itself should not be trusted. The evidence, though unadulterated, may in fact be ambiguous. And any single reading may have suffered alteration that disguises, distorts, or even reverses the direction of variation, as, for example, through coincidence in error in separate versions, or through correction. The more important and significant a reading is for the meaning of the text, the more liable are variants to be tampered with. The most reliable type of evidence of direction of variation is provided by the more unobtrusive and yet identifiable errors, or best of all by normally irreversible deficiencies such as missing lines or pairs of lines, where the error or absence is revealed only by the existence of a version or versions with a better text. The safe rule is never to infer direction of variation from only one or two indicative readings. All the variant readings that can be analysed to show direction of variation should be taken account of, and as far as possible treated separately, so that any inconsistency in the pattern will be shown up. If the textual materials provide only one or two distinctive variants, then suitable caution must be exercised, and any doubts about the validity of the results must be passed on to the reader.

The method just described of identifying direction of variation by deciding the priority in time of certain variants would seem to short-cut the whole process of establishing a stemma and make it depend on a couple of subjective judgments. Worse still, the argument appears to be circular: we are anticipating what we are ultimately trying to prove, namely the priority of readings, in order to establish the priority of versions that will enable us to judge the priority of readings. There is truth in this objection as far as it goes, but not so as to undermine the validity of the procedure, if the following distinctions and safeguards are borne in mind. We are not assuming the absolute rightness or wrongness of the variants we take as indicators of direction of variation, but simply the priority in time of one with respect to another. Both (all) may be wrong with respect to the author's original reading or even with respect to some other extant reading. Nor are we trusting to these few indicative variants and deficiencies for establishing the full stemma; they are used only as a guide to direction of variation. The inevitable element of subjectivity here and in other stages of textual analysis is controlled by the total methodology that minimizes the possibility of fallacious deduction.

We need to stress the greater importance of the version at this stage than of the individual readings and their variants. A text is, of course, a congeries of individual readings, and the aim of the process of textual criticism is to select the individual readings that will make up the final text. Also the individual variants are what enable us to retrace genealogy. In seeking to establish the stemma, however, we do not trust ourselves to individual variants. Individual variants may have a history different from that of the version and so be no guide to the treatment of other readings in the text. Thus, as we shall see, we register *all* the variants for the whole text, major and trivial, authentic and unauthentic alike, and we analyse them not individually but collectively, not in isolation but in combination, because even when the history of some individual variants is erratic, the version as a whole retains the distinctive patterns of original text and accumulated variants that attest its genealogy. The focus is on the relatively stable and reliable matrix and not on the individual variants. Nor is it a matter of rigidly and exclusively following one line of procedure to the end in isolation from all other considerations. The stemma is deduced and confirmed by various lines of analysis that proceed *pari passu*. What might be suggested by grouping of variants alone is controlled by evidence of direction of variation; what might be inferred from one pattern of variants has to be balanced against what seems to be implied by the pattern of other variants, and a hypothesis has to be framed that will accommodate all the principal evidence of whatever sort. When the pattern of relationships is elicited, as far as may be, any anomalies and special cases can be identified and discussed, but *as anomalies* within the overall picture provided by the stemma, which records the genetic relationships of versions and not of variants. Then when we proceed to make the final text, the stemmatic relationships of the versions control much of what we do. Some variants are self-authenticating, obviously 'right', and require no further validation, but there are many more readings whose authenticity, if it can be determined at all, can only be assessed by using a stemma. And any special manipulation of readings or emendation of transmitted text have to be seen in the light of the history and relationships of the versions of the text as summarized in the stemma.

Supplementary notes:

Variant can be used of any characteristic of a version that differs from the equivalent characteristic of another version by addition, alteration, or omission. The types of variant (wording, spelling, punctuation, lay-out, etc.) that the critic regards as worthy of note will change according to his aims and purposes, but generally the word is applied to those differences that affect the actual substance of the text and its interpretation. See further in the note on *Version*.

The term 'variant' by itself contains no presumption about the relationship between the different readings: whether one is 'correct' and another 'incorrect', one 'earlier' and another 'later', or whether indeed the readings have a direct relationship with each other at all. Variant readings are simply different. Often, however, the word is used with an implication of direction of change away from an original, as when we say 'a variant was introduced in copy A'. In this sense variants are readings which do not accord with the author's original, or do not accord with the lineal version, principally as found in the copy-text. Both senses of 'variant' are sanctioned by usage, so editors must always recognize in which sense they are using the word and beware of using it with an unjustified presumption about the direction of variation.

Variation may not always be visible when the variants of a particular reading are looked at in isolation from their versions. If an author's reading is distorted in version P and then restored in a subsequent version Q, Q's reading will not show up as a variant. In terms of textual transmission, however, both changes constitute variation, as would appear when the history of the transmission of the versions was known.

As far as lines of descent are concerned, our primary interest is in 'variation' and not 'correctness'. But if correction has taken place, this is of interest to the editor as possible evidence of the care and intelligence of the copyist who transmitted a particular version — or of his cavalier attitude to copy-text — and may influence the editor's assessment of the value of other readings in that version.

See Greg for a description of complex variants and their resolution.

Version is used of a body of text with intrinsic features that differentiate it from other forms of the same body of text. This broad definition will serve for most purposes without further refinement. The general notion is often all that is required, and the context will indicate the appropriate range of meaning. But the concept has complexities that may not be obvious, and clarity of ideas is very important here, because attention centres on the version, as already explained on pages 38-39.

In the most general sense each and every copy of a text which has a distinguishing feature is a 'version'. But not all such versions have the same status for the textual critic. In the first place, his specialized needs will largely exclude versions that result from substantial revision, adaptation, or rewriting.[15] An excellent

15. Here lies a particular problem for the editor of play-texts. As we have already noted (page 30), plays may be modified for or in performance, and this with (in descending order) the author's cooperation, approval, or permission. Authors themselves revised their work for performance and for publication, and also sanctioned published texts tidied up by others. With such possibilities, which in any case we may have no means of recognizing or even knowing of, the 'author's original' may seem a chimera. Nonetheless, provided we do not forget that the author's original may not be a simple, single version, we can use the term in a general discussion such as this as shorthand for the ideal goal of textual criticism. If more than one revision or state of the work being edited is extant, the most sensible way of proceeding will be dictated by the nature of the case. For the editor as literary critic and historian, of course, all revisions and adaptations are of interest. See also note 6, and above, page 34.

example is the *Tan largo* version of Tirso's *El burlador de Sevilla*. The usefulness of such versions will be in proportion to the degree to which they reproduce or reflect the version used as base, the text the editor is concerned to edit. Nevertheless, even where the degree of correspondance between modified and unmodified texts is so small that the modified text has little value for stemmatic recension, it may still help in confirming individual readings or features of the unmodified text known from other extant versions, and may help with emendations. But the editor will proceed with due caution, remembering that he is dealing with a modified text which may not be a sincere witness.

Revisions apart, two other broad senses of version may be distinguished. The first may be called the *terminal version*. These are the actual versions that resulted from the decision to copy a certain body of text (the reason for this phrasing will become clear), the versions that are or were found in specific copies. When made, they came at the end of a line of transmission of the text, hence 'terminal'. Each one is textually unique (we are not concerned with scribal peculiarities, variant spellings, etc., that do not affect the text itself): mostly the version will reproduce its copy-text, but textual variants peculiar to this copy are also introduced. (For exceptions see note 14.) However, not all the new variants are of the same sort, and not all occur at the same time. There are those unintentional variants that occur during the initial act of copying, such as misspellings, misunderstandings, accidental omissions, and unconscious alterations of one sort or another; in addition in printers' copies there are variants related to the technicalities of printing: foul case, turned letters, etc. There are also intentional variants, which again may occur during the primary act of copying, but may also be introduced later: running corrections of copying errors in MSS, corrections of what are thought to be errors in the copy-text, 'improvements', cuts, and in printed texts the stop-press corrections and alterations that produce the different states of a single edition. Also occurring over a span of time are physical loss and damage to copies, including in this category damage occurring during the print-run of printed texts — type-batter, slipping type, etc. In view of these complications we need to refine the definition of 'terminal version'.

The terminal version can be regarded as that produced as the immediate fulfilment of the desire to copy a certain text; it is a) what the copyist actually puts on paper or sets in type, with b) the corrections that belong to this primary intent of copying, when they can be certainly identified as such — in the case of MS copies the visible corrections, both running corrections and later, and in printed editions the stop-press corrections — and c) discounting for textual purposes all such obvious errors remaining in the copy as show clearly what the copyist's intention was and therefore are certain to be corrected by any reader or copyist. ('Corrections' of the copy-text, whether deliberate or unconscious, that the copyist incorporates in his version are regarded simply as readings of the terminal version. When by some means we can discern features of a lost copy-text, as, for example, by compositor analysis, we are uncovering a previous terminal version, and not a state of the extant version.) Changes made to the copy subsequently that do not belong to this primary act of copying, including changes due to physical deterioration, can be regarded as producing *states* of the terminal version rather than new versions. Similarly, uncorrected text before corrections of the type listed under b) have been made, and which may on occasion be used as copy-text, can be regarded as an uncorrected state of the terminal version. Of course states can be separated only when we have appropriate evidence: either, in MSS, deletions, inks, handwriting, etc., or copies of a printed edition that preserve the different states, or information in the extant textual materials that enables us to infer states in lost terminal versions. And even in the case of an extant MS there can be difficulty in telling whether a particular alteration belongs to an earlier or a later state of the version. The editor simply has to adapt to the circumstances and provide *ad hoc* explanations as required. It is not an exact science. The only terminal versions we usually need to concern ouselves with are the extant versions.

The second category of version may be called the *lineal version*. All the copies that derive from a particular version, whether directly or through intermediate copies, are witnesses to their ancestral version. (Again, for the sake of simplicity, we ignore the possible complications.) Each new copy will modify the text it receives, and yet, although the witnesses may become progressively more unreliable, distinctive features of the ancestral version will remain. Thus we can talk of the lineal version transmitted through a whole branch or line of a stemma. For the textual critic the most important lineal versions are those deriving from the exclusive common ancestors of extant versions.

When any copyist or editor, ancient or modern, deliberately seeks to restore the text, his target is what he conceives to be the lineal version. Indeed it could be said that the notional target for any copyist, whatever his degree of integrity or commitment, is always the lineal version rather than the terminal version that provides the copy-text. That is why he makes spontaneous corrections. Note that any extant version may for textual purposes be treated as a lineal version if it is the sole witness.

Version and copy. From various points in the preceding discussion it will be seen that the notion of 'version' can be separated from the notion of 'copy', both in the bibliographical sense of the specific piece of paper or collection of papers (or other medium) carrying text (the vehicle, as it were), and in the sense of the particular manifestation of text carried in the bibliographical copy (the witness). Such a separation can often be useful, and is sometimes necessary. The editor as historian will be interested in the copy as such — its date and origin, paper and ink, calligraphy or printer's materials, characteristic spellings, its owners, the accidents that befell it, and so on. The textual critic works primarily with versions and not with copies; he is interested in copies only insofar as they bear witness to the text or affect the transmission of the text. Nevertheless it is convenient and usually harmless to give copies and their associated versions the same sigla: version A has as its sole or prime witness copy A.

Independent versions are those which do not derive from another extant version. Unless there has been conflation or correction, a version which is not independent has little value for textual criticism, because its ancestor is available. The later version can in fact be regarded as a state of the version it derives from. We can suspect that an extant version is not independent when the total number of variants peculiar to it alone (Greg's *type-one* variants) is very small. The similar versions should be thoroughly checked to ascertain their true relationship.

IV

How should the editor of a text in multiple versions set about his task of textual criticism? Leaving aside all general questions, such as the nature of a critical text and its apparatus, and all procedures that apply to the editing of any text, we shall concentrate on what concerns stemmatic recension. The fundamental importance of stemmatic recension has already been made clear, as has the fact that it is not a panacea: editors will use other techniques as appropriate, and stemmatic recension will not always be practicable or always solve particular problems. I have tried to avoid repeating previous definitions and explanations, but they must be borne in mind. Along with the essential stages of stemmatic procedure I have given some practical suggestions for handling the materials, although in fact probably every editor develops a *modus operandi* that suits him best.

1. Give all the extant versions a single identification letter (siglum). These can be in alphabetical order or chosen to match some feature of the version (e.g. its origin, copyist, printer, owner, or location).[16] Without alteration type out in full and well spaced any convenient version of the text, preferably the one that appears to be the most complete. Number the lines. Note on the typed copy all peculiarities of the version and its copy that may be of interest (e.g. corrections, copyist's marks, changes of handwriting, illegibilities, physical damage), and any pertinent observations or explanations.

2. Compare in turn each of the other versions with the typed master copy and note all significant variants. Normally variants in spelling (including abbreviations), punctuation, layout, scribal peculiarities, etc., are not significant; if any do appear

---

16. Wherever possible the editor must at some point fully examine the originals of his extant versions. Photocopies cannot reveal all that will be evident to first-hand inspection.

worthy of record, the corresponding variants of all the other versions must be noted. Recording unnecessary details does no harm, but omitting versions from the record of a particular set of variants can produce confusing anomalous groups. As with the master copy, note all peculiarities, etc. The record of variants is best laid out in vertical parallel columns, one column to each version, corresponding line by line to the master copy. Only readings that differ from the master copy need be noted.

3. For each set of variants group the versions according to shared readings and note the sigla of the groups in a final column opposite in the form AB : CDE, or AB : CD : E, etc. Type-one variants can be registered with their single letter (A, or B, etc.). Compound variants, where more than one element of a word or phrase or other brief discrete unit of text has varied independently, require a formula for each element (e.g. *solo diga un pensamiento* : *selo diga el pensamiento* might be *solo* A *un* : *el* ABC : DE). When possible, complex variants, where a particular element has more than two variant forms, should be analysed to reveal latent as well as actual groups. For example, *un pensamiento* : *el pensamiento* : *es pensamiento* might be ABC : DE : F; but we may assume at this stage that the variants *es* and *el* are related: the one might come from the other, but not from *un*; so there is a latent group DEF. The record of the variant will read ABC : DE : F, also DE(F). F will count as a type-one variant. We might learn later that version F is not in fact related to DE; in which case we explain the anomalous group DE(F) as coincidence and discount it. If the versions were grouped *un* : *el* : *es* ABCD : E : F, the record would also note the group E(F), and both E and F would count as type-one variants.

4. On a separate sheet of paper make a register of all the groups that have occurred, actual and latent, and beside them the line-references to where they appear. Latent groups should be clearly marked as such. As an index of locations of groups this register will save hours of hunting in the lists of variants when cross-checking groups, analysing anomalies, etc. It also presents, almost at a glance, the overall pattern of the groups of versions that share variants.

Since we are principally interested in true genetic groups, those with an exclusive common ancestor, ideally the register should record only these groups and not their misleading complement. Where possible, therefore, list variants under groups that can be identified as genetic by exclusively sharing evident deficiencies at certain points in the text. For example, all variants whose full notation was AB : CDE would be listed only as AB variants or as CDE variants, depending on which was the genetic group. When complementary groups each have at different points altered readings with respect to the other (as with DE and GHI in Stemma 3), the variants can be listed under either group, but with a note that the complementary group is also apparently a genetic group. If neither of two complementary groups ever has obvious deficiencies with respect to the other, and if the direction of variation is not clear from other evidence, then either group can be recorded or both. This is often the case with minor groups, that is, groups that seldom occur. Major groups, those that occur most often, are more likely to reveal whether or not they are genetic groups. If it becomes clear later that the group listed is only the complement of a genetic group, the genetic group can be substituted. But check all the references to ensure that the group now listed actually occurs every time. For example, the normal complement of ABC may be DE, but for a particular reading it may be D : E.

Complex variants of the type AB : C : DE should be recorded under all their elements, with a note each time that the variant is complex. All type-one variants can be listed simply as A, or B, etc. At most only one of their complementary groups is likely to be a genetic group, as, for example, BCD in Stemma 5 (the

Stemma 5

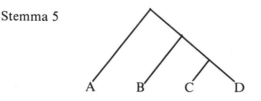

A   B   C   D

complement of A). If a version has very few type-one variants, check that it really is independent.

The register of groups must be comprehensive, that is, it must record all obviously or potentially significant groups that occur. Annotations and explanations should be written in as necessary. If obvious errors and deficiencies in the versions are marked in red on the register and any apparently good readings are marked in green, some of the anomalous groups and readings that always occur will be instantly identifiable (others may be discovered later), and the confirmation of genetic groups will be obvious. In the fortunate circumstance that all major groups in the register are indeed genetic, then direction of variation is, as it were, built into the register.

5. Attempts at drawing a stemma can now be made. Normally all but one of the sets of type-one variants can be excluded; see above, section 4. Always bearing in mind the direction of variation, begin with the groups that occur most often, the major groups. If major groups overlap (e.g. ABCD, BCD, and CD), take the groups with least members first (the example will produce Stemma 5). When a stemma, or provisional stemma, has been drawn that will account for the existence of the major groups and their direction of variation, the minor groups can be tackled. Watch out for minor groups that are merely major groups with one or more members missing (e.g. BC might be BCD with separate variation in D). With the register of groups in front of him the editor will soon come to recognize the kinds of manipulation that will coordinate and simplify the materials.

Only at this point can inconsistent groups and anomalous readings be properly identified. All such detectable incongruities (there are almost bound to be others not now detectable) must be assessed and, if possible, explained, in the light of the general relationships of the versions revealed by the major groups and compatible minor groups. What precisely caused particular groups and readings inconsistent with the stemma to appear is often difficult to tell. The possible causes may be so numerous that speculation is unprofitable or pointless. In my experience, however, texts in multiple versions *normally* have some readings and minor groups that do not fit the stemma. The likeliest explanation therefore in most cases is not conflation (the deliberate introduction into a version of variant readings from another version that is being compared with it) but chance coincidence (e.g. through polygenesis of common error or independent spontaneous correction) or contamination (e.g. when a copyist who knew another version from reading or performance either consciously or unconsciously introduced a reading from that source or influenced by it). Before we use conflation as an explanation, there must be weighty internal or external evidence pointing to deliberate intervention.

Conflation and contamination should both be distinguished from the independent use of more than one copy-text, particularly when two or more copyists or compositors are working together. If the component sections of the resulting composite version can be adequately separated, they should be treated as fragmentary copies of their respective lineal versions. The Pando editions of several of Calderón's *autos* are identifiably composite versions, and they also show a sometimes considerable amount of editorial intervention that includes conflation of the different copy-texts.

Each text is likely to throw up its own stemmatic problems. The general principles already given are a foundation on which to build. Beyond that, much depends on the experience and ingenuity of the editor — and his friends.

Before we move on to the final section, we need to be quite clear about what exactly a stemma records. It presents schematically the fundamental genetic relationships between the extant versions of a text — versions rather than copies (see the notes on *Version* and *Version and copy*, pages 40-43), although the distinction cannot be pressed absolutely. We infer from the extant versions the existence of other versions, their exclusive common ancestors (the inferential versions), and ignore possible intermediate versions (the potential versions). The stemma is thus not necessarily the full genealogical record of the versions of the text, or a complete history of its transmission. The stemma might even be regarded as more a logical than a genealogical diagram, and we might prefer, as some do, to replace the category of 'ancestor' with that of 'archetype'. The position of extant versions in the stemma provides in itself no evidence about the comparative reliability of the extant versions, although it would show, for example, that an obviously badly corrupt version must be given due consideration because it is the sole witness of a particular branch of the textual family (like copy D in Stemma 4). Nor does the stemma show the chronological order in which independent extant copies were made.

If the versions are independent, chronological precedence is irrelevant, and only the genetic relationships count. For other precautions to bear in mind when reading a stemma see again section III.

6. The initial selection of readings for the final text depends on a thorough and dispassionate exploitation of the information the stemma can provide. First adopt from the extant versions the readings which, on stemmatic evidence, are necessarily or (more realistically) in all probability those of the earliest common ancestor, which we will call X. These readings will be attested throughout the stemma by at least two out of three or more extant or lineal versions sharing an exclusive common ancestor, or by both versions, if there are only two. These are *confirmed readings*. When the stemma is reduced to two lineal versions, a reading attested by only one of the two witnesses of X may seem to be self-authenticating, but such readings really belong with those dealt with in the next paragraph. At all points the editor must be careful not to misjudge the evidential value of readings that are anomalous within the patterns of the stemma. Unless the extant witnesses are exceedingly corrupt, or the textual transmission is unusually tangled, these confirmed readings of X should make up most of the final text.

Secondly, when the stemmatic evidence is inconclusive or is reduced to two lineal versions witnessing to X, the editor may still with some degree of confidence be able to discriminate between variants. One variant may be intrinsically more acceptable than the others, or may be left as the only reasonable choice because the other variants are unacceptable. The criteria of acceptability will include the demands of sense and metre, stylistic considerations, and consistency with the author's known habits of thought or expression. Again try to identify readings that the stemma shows are later sophistications of the transmitted text. Readings need not be rejected on that count alone, but the editor must point out when such readings are accepted.

The first stage of stemmatic recension has established as objectively as possible the originality or unoriginality (as readings of X) of a large number of variants. The proportion of definitely original variants in the different versions can be calculated and the quotient used as a check against indefensible editorial bias when choosing 'acceptable' readings in the second stage. The results of these two stages can then be added together to provide an index of probability that can guide the editor in choosing from among the remaining variants. This is Greg's 'calculus of variants', slightly adapted.

Thirdly, there remain the readings with *indeterminate variants*, where a choice cannot be made by using the stemma or on the ground of their obvious acceptability or unacceptability. Indeterminate variants can be of three sorts. (i) A variant from one of the lines of descent may give a reading which is more subtle or enriches the sense or expression in some way. The *enriching variants* should be chosen and the weaker variants rejected, unless there are special reasons to the contrary. This procedure can be defended on the ground that spontaneous variation more commonly emasculates a text than improves it. There is obviously no independent guarantee of the authenticity of such readings; only probability favours them. But we also honour the author in preferring enriching variants. (ii) Where there is no obvious advantage in choosing one indeterminate variant rather than another, they can be called *neutral variants*. The choice of reading should be influenced first by the calculus of variants and then by any other relevant indication. An explanatory note must identify all such readings, so that the user of the edition is aware of viable alternatives. (iii) The residue of indeterminate readings are those in which all the variants are for some reason unsatisfactory or *dubious*. These should be treated as neutral variants, but should be separately identified.

X will now have been reconstructed to the extent possible using only readings preserved in the extant versions. At any stage in the preparation of the final text, however, the editor may be led by internal or external evidence to question and emend transmitted readings, and may thus arrive at a better reconstruction of X, or even recover still earlier authorial readings, if X is not itself an authorial version. Emendation is a separate and important subject, which cannot be dealt with here. Some elementary principles can be found in my 'Métodos de crítica textual', page 17, note 3. The safest general rule is to interfere as little as possible with the readings of X preserved in the extant versions. Greater liberties can be taken with stage directions. Not being part of the spoken text, and not always even being regarded as essential to the play, stage directions were frequently abbreviated or modified in successive versions, or omitted altogether. As already noted (above, page 31), stage directions also move from their appropriate place in relation to the text. The editor should familiarize himself with the normal practice and terminology of the author, as far as evidence is available, and then, bearing these in mind, reconstruct from the extant versions the fullest stage direction and place it where most suitable. Additional directions, properly identified, can be added.

The mechanical application of stemmatic methods does not, as it were, automatically generate the final text. The editor not the method produces the final text, which will always have the imprimatur of editorial judgment. Since the degree of confidence that can be placed in the different readings will vary according to the basis on which each was chosen, the editor must provide appropriate annotation to guide the user of his edition.

The constant need for vigilance and for flexibility limit the usefulness of computers in textual criticism, although much work has been done on the problems involved.[17] Extensive pre-editing and sophisticated coding of texts are necessary before the computer can perform any useful manipulation of the data. And it is precisely at this level of actually examining copies, and thinking about and questioning the primary textual materials that most of the editor's discoveries are made. Preparing the materials for electronic manipulation simply doubles the task to no advantage. A better aid is a set of coloured pens and highlighters. Computers, or more conveniently word processors, do have obvious value in storing and reproducing data, and in preparing the final copy of the critical text accompanied by its apparatus.

17. Current bibliography can be found in issues of *Computers and the Humanities*.

THE EDITING OF SPANISH GOLDEN-AGE PLAYS FROM EARLY PRINTED VERSIONS

Don W. Cruickshank

The transmission of a text is not necessarily a process of continuous corruption and the introduction of errors. Corrections can be introduced by editors, copyists or compositors at almost any stage. These corrections may be made up (and so lacking in authority), or they may derive from another, more correct version. Corrections added to a manuscript or to a printed book after its production can usually be detected without difficulty; but if the corrected copy is used to produce a new manuscript or a new printed edition, the process of correction will be concealed, the identity of the corrector obscured, and the reliability of his corrections made uncertain.

An editor needs to discover as much as possible about the hidden areas of the transmission process. Unless he does, he will never know how close he has got to his ultimate aim, which is 'to produce the text as finally approved by the author'. One says 'how close' advisedly, for the ultimate aim will often be unattainable. There will frequently be an unbridgeable gap between the manifestly defective surviving version and the version which the author must have produced.[1] In other cases, the editor's path to the 'finally-approved' text may branch in several directions: to one or more manuscripts partly or wholly in the author's hand, and/or to one or more printed editions corrected (or possibly corrected) by the author.[2]

In the case of printed sources, the editor's task may be divided into seven different (though often closely related) parts. He will have to:

1. Trace surviving editions and investigate relationships between them.
2. Identify as far as possible those versions of his text which must have existed but which are lost.
3. Identify the version to be used as the basis for his edition (the 'copy-text').
4. Identify other versions which might be used to correct flaws in the copy-text.
5. Decide what kind of edition to produce, given the nature of the copy-text and of other useful texts.
6. Decide how much, and what kind of critical apparatus to include.
7. Do the actual editing, with the many minor decisions which that involves.

Some of these parts are far more complex than others. The fifth and sixth ones are as likely, nowadays, to be influenced by financial as by scholarly considerations. Even the first one may be affected by the availability of funds. However, the suggestions which follow are intended to be governed only by scholarly principles. Editors must make up their own minds about cutting their coats to fit their cloth.

1. One thinks of *El burlador de Sevilla* and *Tan largo me lo fiais*; these are often said to be independent descendants of a lost original, but if they are, they vary so greatly that it will be almost impossible to reconstruct the original.

2. Lope's *El castigo sin venganza* survives in an autograph manuscript of 1631 and in an edition, apparently prepared by Lope, of Barcelona, 1634; they vary. Calderón's *El postrer duelo de España* survives in three manuscripts, one of which has portions in Calderón's hand, as well as in editions of 1672 and 1674, in the second of which the plays are allegedly 'enmendadas, y corregidas'. Again, the versions vary.

If financial considerations affect the production of modern editions of Golden-Age plays, they affected the production of the original ones even more. Both the theatre and the book trade were businesses, run by professionals out to make money. The dramatists were still amateurs by modern standards, but they soon discovered that it was better to write with performance than publication in mind: a stage manager would pay from 500 to 1000 *reales* (or more) for a play, while a publisher might baulk at 100.[3] As a result, plays were rarely published until their performing potential was exhausted — a process which might take years. During such a long period, many things might happen to the text of a play. The companies of actors who 'owned' plays were under no obligation to perform them as the author had written them. They might make modifications: excisions, additions or revisions, depending to some extent on the abilities of the actors involved. The author himself might be involved in modifications, either because he kept in touch with the actors who had bought his play, or because he took the trouble to keep or acquire a copy of it to publish himself.[4]

There was money to be made in publishing plays, but not much. Profit margins were small, so that unless they were subsidised, printers and publishers had little incentive to try to restore a battered text to some semblance of correctness, or even to do what their technology permitted to preserve a correct one from error.

'To do what their technology permitted' is an important phrase: unless he has a grasp of the limits and potential of Golden-Age printing technology, the editor is not equipped to tackle his job. We must examine that technology before going any further.

Books of the sixteenth and seventeenth centuries were not

3. See H. A. Rennert, *The Spanish Stage in the Time of Lope de Vega* (New York, 1909), pp. 177-8, for prices paid by stage managers. It is hard to discover what a publisher would have paid for a new play, since new plays were almost never sold for publication. William Byron, in his *Cervantes: A Biography* (London, 1979), pp. 414, 482, quotes some of the fees paid by publishers for prose works (Cervantes's *Novelas ejemplares* and *Galatea*, Rojas Villandrando's *Viaje entretenido* and Espinel's *Marcos de Obregón*): they range from 1100 to 1600 *reales*. If comparable sums were paid for volumes of plays, their value to a publisher was about 90 to 130 *reales* each. The price paid for Cervantes's *Ocho comedias, y ocho entremeses nuevos, nunca representados* is not known, but is reckoned to have been much less than the 1600 *reales* he got for the *Novelas ejemplares*.

4. One unambiguous example of a late revision is *El mayor monstruo los celos*, printed in 1637, but surviving in a manuscript in which Calderón's revision can be dated by handwriting changes to *circa* 1670.

produced as a series of single leaves, but as a series of large sheets of paper, each of them folded to make two, four, eight or more leaves. this is still the commonest way of making books, but many features have changed. Before 1550, Spanish plays were most commonly printed in folio format. After that date quarto prevailed, and eventually became almost universal. The terms 'folio', 'quarto', etc., refer to the number of leaves produced by folding the original sheet of paper once (folio, two leaves), twice (quarto, four leaves), three times (octavo, eight leaves) or four times (sextodecimo or sixteenmo, sixteen leaves). Their abbreviations are 2°, 4°, 8°, 16°. When a modern compositor sets a book, he begins at the beginning and goes on until he reaches the end. This did not become usual until the nineteenth century, because printing houses did not have enough type for a complete book, unless it was very short. Spanish printing-houses were particularly short of type in the seventeenth century: many had enough type of a given size for only eight quarto pages, or even less. As a result, production of a book did not involve the setting of the text, followed by the printing of the text, but the setting of a small portion of the text, which was then printed so that the type could be distributed to set the next portion of the text, and so on.

If the printer had enough type to set eight quarto pages, he could set them in their proper order: 1 (folio 1^r), 2 (1^v), 3 (2^r), 4 (2^v), 5 (3^r), 6 (3^v), 7 (4^r). At this point, after only seven pages, he had enough to print one side of his first sheet of paper. In a simple quarto book, the inside of the first sheet, when folded, contains pages, 2, 3, 6, 7. It is known as the inner forme, and since its setting was usually completed before that of the outer forme, it was generally printed first. This straightforward, seriatim method of setting the text is called 'setting by pages'. Once printed, the two sides of the first sheet of the book would look like this:

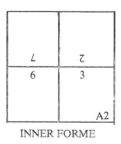

L	Z		S	t
6	3		8	1
	A2			A

INNER FORME   OUTER FORME

As a guide principally for the binder, the compositor would put a 'signature' at the bottom right of the first odd-numbered page (the first recto) of each forme, in the order A, A2, A3, A4, etc. Thus in a simple quarto book the first leaf will be signed A, the second A2; sometimes the third leaf (the second recto of the outer forme) is signed A3; exceptionally rarely the fourth leaf (se second recto of the inner forme) is also signed, A4. The fifth leaf, as part of a new sheet, will be B, the sixth B2, and so on through the twenty-three letter alphabet (excluding J, U, W). If there are more than twenty-three sheets, the twenty-fourth will be signed Aa, the next Aa2, the forty-seventh Aaa, the next Aaa2, etc.[5]

A printer who lacked the type to set seven or eight quarto pages seriatim would 'cast off' parts of his text to set a forme. Casting off a verse play was easy, and merely involved counting lines and allowing for stage directions. Casting off prose required more care and experience. A compositor who wanted to set the first sheet of a play in quarto format by this method would cast off page 1, set pages 2 and 3, cast off 4 and 5, and set 6 and 7; this would complete the inner forme, at the cost of casting off three pages. It was possible to set page 1 first, cast off 2 and 3, set 4 and 5, cast off 6 and 7, and finally set 8, which would complete the outer forme, but only at the cost of four cast-off pages. Consequently, the printers' normal practice when using the casting-off method was to set the inner forme first, and so it would usually be printed first, just as it was in the 'setting by pages' method. The correct name of the casting-off method is 'setting by formes'. It was slower than setting by pages because of the time spent casting off, and Christophe Plantin, an efficient printer with plenty of type, abandoned it in the 1560s. In Spain the method persisted throughout most of the seventeenth century, probably because Spanish printers of this period were chronically short of type.[6]

So much for 'simple quarto' (Spanish *cuarto sencillo*), properly called 'quarto in fours' in English; it was virtually the

5. For further information on how books were made, see P. Gaskell, *A New Introduction to Bibliography* (Oxford, 1972); for the terminology of descriptive bibliography, see F. Bowers, *Principles of Bibliographical Description* (Princeton, 1949).

6. Gaskell, *A New Introduction*, p. 42 (Plantin); D. W. Cruickshank, 'Some Aspects of Spanish Book-production in the Golden Age', *The Library*, V, 31 (1976), 3, n. 11. To distinguish between setting by formes and setting by pages, one must check the recurrence of identifiable pieces of type; see D. W. Cruickshank, 'The Printing of Calderón's *Tercera parte*', *SB*, 23 (1970), 230-51.

standard format for printing single plays in Spain from about 1670 to almost 1850. In the first half of the seventeenth century the standard format was the more complex 'quarto in eights' (*cuarto conjugado*), which was used for both single plays and collected volumes. In the quarto in fours the binder's unit (a 'gathering' or 'quire') was one sheet; in the quarto in eights the gathering had two sheets; both were folded twice, then one was placed inside the second fold of the other. This practice halved the amount of sewing and made it easier to bind long books without bulky spines. It made life harder for the printers, however, for few of them had enough type to set a quarto in eights by pages; setting by formes (with correspondingly more casting off) was almost always necessary. The diagrams below show the layout of the pages.

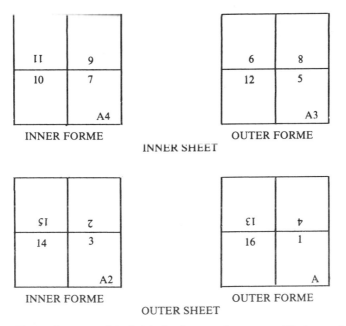

Experiment with folded pieces of paper will show that the inner forme of the inner sheet could be set by casting off seven pages; the outer forme of the same sheet required eight pages to be cast off; and the inner and outer formes of the outer sheet involved eleven and twelve cast-off pages respectively. That is why the formes of a quarto in eights were usually set (and printed) in the order in which they appear in the diagrams above. This also explains why printers who were setting from an earlier edition (as opposed to a manuscript) would often follow the layout of the earlier edition page for page: it saved time and avoided mistakes in casting off.[7]

Once the compositor had set the four pages of his first quarto forme, he would lay them out ('impose' them) in the appropriate order on the imposing stone. Round the pages would be laid the chase, a rectangular iron frame. The pages were kept separate from each other and from the inside edges of the chase by wooden 'furniture'. Type and furniture were locked tight by driving in wooden wedges between furniture and chase. It is important to remember that the quarto forme of type, with its four pages, was a mirror-image of the pages as they were to appear on the printed sheet.

When the forme was imposed, the compositor would take it to the pressmen, who would take the first proof, using scrap paper and (very often) an old press kept for the purpose. The first proof might be examined for 'literals' (single wrong letters) by the compositor himself. This process could be done without reference to the copy. The compositor could also give the proof and the relevant part of the copy to a corrector, who would examine the proof while a reading boy read aloud to him from the copy. In this way the corrector could follow the words of the text (the substantives) as they were read to him, while checking that the compositor had supplied or normalised the accidentals (punctuation, spelling, capitalisation, etc.). The reading boy might mention

7. The easiest way to identify the format of a Spanish book is by its size. Almost all ordinary Spanish books were printed on foolscap, which was about 44 by 31 cm. Each successive fold halved the longer dimension, so that folio was 31 by 22, quarto 22 by 15.5, octavo 15.5 by 11 and so on. After trimming, these dimensions would be 30 by 21, 21 by 14.5 and 15 by 10.5 cm. approximately. Thus a folio will be about 12 inches tall, a quarto just over 8 inches and an octavo not quite 6 inches. If doubt still remains, the paper must be examined to establish the direction of the chain-lines and the position of the watermarks (if any): see Gaskell, *A New Introduction*, pp. 60-77, 84-6. The final gathering of a quarto in eights will often consist of more or less than two complete sheets, e.g. Z^6, Z^{10}, Z^{12}; that is, 1½ sheets, 2½ sheets, 3 sheets. Investigators will find it easy to draw diagrams of the formes involved if they remember that the half sheet was always innermost in the gathering. Thus the outermost sheet of a Z^{10} gathering will have 1^v, 2^r, 9^v, 10^r as its inner forme, 1^r, 2^v, 9^r, 10^v as its outer. The middle sheet will have 3^v, 4^r, 7^v, 8^r and 3^r, 4^v, 7^r, 8^v. The innermost (half) sheet will have 5^v, 6^r and 5^r, 6^v.

some of the more notable accidentals in the copy, but he would not mention all of them. In any case, manuscript copy tended to have scanty punctuation and irregular spelling and capitalisation. It was the compositor's task to bring these accidentals up to an acceptable standard, and the task of the corrector to see that he had done so. Both would be influenced by the accidentals of the copy, especially if it were printed.

When the proof-reading was complete and the errors marked, the compositor would correct the type, following the indications of the corrector. A second proof might then be taken to verify that the corrections had been properly made. If the author or another outsider were involved in correction, it would usually be at this stage, but he would almost always have to be present in the printing-house; the modern practice of sending proofs to an author or editor caused too great a delay in the printing process to be practicable. If the second proof was satisfactory, the presswork would begin; if not, further corrections might be made and a third proof taken.[8] However, the manner in which Golden-Age plays usually reached the printers (years after their authors had sold them for performance) had the effect of excluding the authors and any others who cared about the correctness of the texts. Few plays can have enjoyed as many as three stages of proofing.

In some (many?) cases, presswork must have started while the last proof was still being read. Thus if we examine several copies of a book, we shall often find differences ('press-variants') between the copies. In a modern printing-house this rarely happens: what are effectively proof sheets are not used in the final book. In Golden-Age Spain, however, the lower standards of printing, combined with pressures on the pressmen both to keep busy and to avoid wasting the expensive paper, meant that this occurred often enough for it to be considered a standard practice.[9]

8. For more details on proofing, see Gaskell, *A New Introduction*, pp. 110-16.

9. For press-variants in Spanish plays, see Cruickshank, 'The Printing of Calderón's *Tercera parte*', 238; and 'The Text of *La vida es sueño*', in *The comedias of Calderón*, edited by D. W. Cruickshank and J. E. Varey, 19 vols. (Farnborough, 1973), I, *The Textual Criticism of Calderón's comedias*, pp. 79-87. The variants described in these articles were discovered by means of a Hinman collating machine, which can collate only originals and good original-size photocopies. More modern aids to collating use TV cameras and can cope with microfilms: John Horden, 'The Institute of Bibliography and Textual Criticism, Leeds', *The Library*, V, 27 (1972), 300-1.

While the first forme was at press, the compositor would start setting the second. In a modest printing-house, he might not have enough type to complete all four pages, and would have to wait for the first forme to be printed so that he could make use of its type. Even in the better firms a compositor would generally have to distribute type from his first forme in order to complete his third one. The implications of this are obvious: the size of an edition (number of copies to be printed) had to be decided at the outset, because it depended on the number of copies printed of the very first forme; if a firm began by printing 1000 copies and later decided that the market could take 1500, it would be necessary to print *from scratch* the extra 500 copies of those sheets already printed. This was so uneconomical that it was rarely done for a volume of plays.

When a forme had been printed, some of the type might not be distributed. The running headlines could be used for the remainder of the play, while recurring titles such as COMEDIA FAMOSA would be needed twelve times in a normal *parte de comedias*. Since much Spanish type of this period was in poor or damaged condition, it is often possible to see damaged letters and titles recurring throughout a book. This can help to prove that the book was (or was not) printed in one printing-house, while the number of different sets of running headlines in use will often reveal how many chases (and therefore, perhaps, how many compositors) were involved in a particular book. (Each quarto forme would have two verso headlines, e.g. *La vida es sueño*, and two recto ones, *De Don Pedro Calderón de la Barca*. A single set of four headlines sufficed for a single chase; two sets would imply two chases, and two chases would point to the availability of a reasonable amount of type, as well as to the possible involvement of two compositors, especially if there were supporting evidence from spelling, etc.)

When the pressmen had printed the first forme, the pile of sheets was turned, and the second forme printed on the blank side. In theory, therefore, the sheets were printed in the same order for both first and second formes; if both formes were corrected during the run, then the first sheets to be printed would have the uncorrected versions on both sides. In practice inconsistent working patterns were common.

The last sheets to be printed were the preliminaries. This was partly because they contained the errata-list and the *tassa*, or price, which was reckoned at so many *maravedís* per sheet, and which therefore depended on the length of the completed book. The *tassa* often carries the latest date of any of the preliminary documents, and is usually taken as the date of publication. In Castile, the other documents were the civil and religious approbations, the civil and religious licences, and the (optional) privilege, a form of copyright normally granted for ten years on payment of a fee.[10]

After all the sheets of a book were printed (and dried, since they were printed while damp to improve the impression), they were taken to the binder, who was usually an employee of the bookseller. At this time booksellers would not bind a whole edition at once: it would be stored in sheets, with copies being bound only as sales required. The binder's method was to lay out the piles of printed sheets in an ordered row, down which he then walked, selecting a sheet from each pile in turn until he had one of each. Thus a particular copy would consist, in theory, of the first, or tenth, or *n*th copy of each sheet to be printed. However, the process of hanging sheets up to dry and of collecting them afterwards, and the practice of binding only small numbers of copies at a time, tended to disrupt this regular pattern.

The pressmen would seldom produce exactly the same number of usable copies of every sheet; the bookseller would be left with several copies of some sheets and none of others. If a new edition was likely, these 'extra' sheets would be kept for use in it. This happened, for example, in Calderón's *Verdadera quinta parte* of 1682 and 1691. The consequences will concern any editor who is making use of a corrected second or subsequent edition: if he does not notice that a sheet or sheets have been incorporated from a previous edition, he may miss some valuable corrections.[11]

10. On the documents of the preliminaries, see J. Moll, 'Problemas bibliográficos del libro del Siglo de Oro', *BRAE*, 59 (1979), 51-7, which also deals briefly with the practice in other Spanish kingdoms; and J. Simón Díaz, *La bibliografía: conceptos y aplicaciones* (Barcelona, 1971), pp. 127-72. Moll's is perhaps the best general introduction to the circumstances peculiar to the production of Spanish books of this period.

11. D. W. Cruickshank, 'Don Juan de Vera Tassis y Villarroel', in *Aureum Saeculum Hispanum. Festschrift für Hans Flasche zu:n 70. Geburtstag*, edited by K.-H. Körner and D. Briesemeister (Wiesbaden, 1983), p. 50. Vera did correct the 1691 edition.

*   *   *   *   *

The possibilities for error at all stages of this long process of production were almost infinite. The compositor might misread his original ('misreading'); or, having read it correctly, might memorise it wrongly, adding, omitting or substituting words ('memorial error'). His eye might be caught, subconsciously, by other, perhaps similar, words or passages in his text, which he might set instead of the original ('eyeskip'). Such mistakes could also cause him to omit words, lines or complete passages, or even to set them twice. He could even forget to turn a leaf of his copy, setting one page twice and omitting another.[12]

The compositor kept his type in a wooden case divided into compartments of various sizes. Type could spill from one compartment into the next, or be placed in the wrong compartment during distribution; this caused the ailment known as 'foul case'. Just as a modern typist may strike the wrong key, the compositor's hand might stray to the wrong compartment ('muscular error'). The composing-stick held only a few lines of type, and accidents might happen as these lines were transferred to the galley, or the galleys to the imposing-stone. Carelessness at this point could cause a whole page or more to fall into 'pie' (chaotic jumble), but often only the outer ends of lines were affected. A minor example might go unnoticed, or might be corrected inadequately.[13]

Most of the errors so far described would be noticed during proofing, but not all. The process of correction could cause fresh errors, or fail to eliminate the old ones. It was easy to make a correction where none was required (i.e. to put it in the wrong place, especially at the ends of lines where the rhyme was the same). And since correction required the removal of the quoins (wedges) from the chase, in order to free the type for manipulation, there were further opportunities for pie or for the undesired movement of type in general. Even if a forme never had its quoins removed during printing, the irregularities of hand-cast type sometimes militated against the successful locking-up of every

12. This is the simplest explanation for what happened on folio 245 of the genuine 1664 edition of Calderón's *Tercera parte*. See M.R. Greer, 'Calderón, Copyists, and the Problem of Endings', *BCom*, 36 (1984), 72-3.

13 Moll, 'Problemas bibliográficos', 70.

piece of type in a forme. Loose pieces tended to adhere to the thick and sticky ink applied by the ink-balls, and were pulled free. Their departure seems often to have gone unremarked, or they might be replaced wrongly. This misfortune could happen at any stage in the printing of a forme. If the removed pieces of type were incorrectly replaced, it might be impossible to distinguish the resulting variant from one involving press-correction.

Even if the compositor set the text correctly, the result could still be ruined by incorrect imposition. Such an error was not always easy to detect in the complex process of setting a quarto in eights. If both formes of a sheet were correctly imposed, it was still possible to produce chaos by turning the sheet wrongly when the time came to print the second side. Sometimes binders were sent instructions which might enable such errors to be patched up; but they did not always heed them.[14]

Of course errors could be put right after printing was completed, if anyone cared enough to insist. A whole sheet could be reprinted. Such a correction cannot be detected unless the paper or type shows some variation from that of the rest of the book, or unless some copy or copies containing the old sheet got through the corrector's net. Other possibilities involved half a sheet or (most common) a single leaf. Again, type or paper may give these away. In a half-sheet of quarto, the chain-lines or watermark in the paper may not match those in the other half of the sheet; in a single quarto leaf this may also be true, but much more obvious will be the fact that the replacement leaf will be glued to the stub of the original one. Such corrections are called 'cancels', whether they involve complete sheets or parts of sheets. Strictly speaking, the incorrect original is the 'cancellandum', the correct new version the 'cancellans'. In some cases a short passage, even a single word would be reprinted in order to be cut out and glued over the original error: this is a 'paste-on cancel'. Since it was not practicable to print pieces of less than half a sheet, smaller cancels would generally be set up more than once so that they could be printed in a sheet, which was cut up afterwards. Thus a single quarto leaf cancel would be set twice; this duplication of the two

14. See D. W. Cruickshank, 'The Textual Criticism of Calderón's *comedias*: A Survey', in *The comedias of Calderón*, I, 25.

pages of the leaf would produce one forme of four pages. The forme would be printed by the work and turn method, and then cut into four. This happened during the printing of the Pando edition of Calderón's *autos*; examination of a number of copies has revealed the presence of two settings of type.[15]

As an alternative to cancels, there was the *fe de erratas*, the errata-list. This was produced by the official corrector. In theory his task was to ensure that no illicit additions were made during printing to the manuscript which had originally been approved. In practice he was reduced to compiling lists of errata. These lists are invariably incomplete — a mere token — and often have errors in page- and line-numbers; they were usually ignored by printers of subsequent editions. However, they may provide an insight into the nature of the original manuscript (except when the corrector did not consult it); and they will very occasionally supply a correct reading that might otherwise have been lost. An editor must be cautious, because some of the 'corrector's' interventions served only to introduce errors.[16]

As a final addendum to this list of potential errors, there may be mentioned that of misbinding. Errors of misbinding will usually affect isolated copies, and should not be confused with errors of imposition, which may have similar results in numbers of copies. They are caused by incorrect folding of the sheets, or by the omission, substitution or incorrect ordering of the sheets.[17]

If the above catalogue of possible mishaps has conveyed the notion that printing standards in Golden-Age Spain were low, then that is appropriate. Standards declined most markedly during the very century in which most of the major plays were written: 1580-1680. They began to recover at the end of the seventeenth century,

---

15. See W. F. Hunter and D. W. Cruickshank, 'Notes on the Text of Calderón's "Psiquis y Cupido para Toledo " ', *Iberoromania*, 4 (1970), 282-4; for other examples of cancels, see Moll, 'Problemas bibliográficos', 70-2. Sometimes when the printers had to produce a *suelta* which required several whole sheets and a quarter sheet, they would set the quarter sheet twice and print it in the manner described for the quarter sheet cancel: see D. W. Cruickshank, 'The First Edition of *El burlador de Sevilla*', *HR*, 49 (1981), 463; *sueltas*, bound by 'stabbing', could cope with a single leaf. As a last resort, the printers could make corrections by hand. Only if these occur in several copies will it be safe to assume that they are the printers'. Even then, they will not always be authoritative.

16. For miscorrections made by the corrector, see E. M. Wilson, 'On the *Tercera parte* of Calderón — 1664', *SB*, 15 (1962), 227-8.

17. See Cruickshank, 'The Textual Criticism of Calderón's *comedias*', p. 12.

and continued to do so until a new height was reached during the Ibarra period, in the 1770s and 1780s, after which they began to fall again. We need not consider the period after 1850, when the traditional way of printing plays in Spain had been abandoned.[18]

The printing trade requires long-term capital investment in order to flourish, and the decline of printing in Spain is directly linked to shortage of investment.[19] The printers' growing indifference to the quality of their product manifested itself in the use of inferior paper, poor ink and worn type. Of course this had the effect of keeping their costs and therefore their prices down. They also adopted means of increasing their turnover: they printed more and more inexpensive *comedias sueltas* in the hope of selling plays to buyers who could not otherwise have afforded them; they also printed large numbers of items they had no legal right to, whether because they were still covered by copyright or because no licence had been obtained. Naturally they made attempts to conceal these illegalities, hoping to deceive the authorities. The result has often been the deception of modern editors.

One of the commonest practices was to publish plays without the author's permission. This was not actually illegal, since the person who paid for a play-text was regarded as the owner. Thus when Vergara Salcedo published Calderón's *Tercera parte* in 1664 without first asking permission, Calderón made some ambiguous remarks, but accepted the volume as his own.[20] Unfortunately, unauthorised publication often led to defective or incorrectly attributed texts. Thus Calderón rejected the 1677 *Quinta parte*, saying that four of its plays were not his, although only two were really by other hands.[21] Publishers with some sort of conscience could avoid direct lies by using such titles as *Seis comedias de Lope de Vega Carpio, y de otros autores* (1603). Only

---

18. For studies on the development of play-printing in Spain, see E. M. Wilson's 'The *comedia suelta*: History of a Format', in E. M. Wilson and D. W. Cruickshank, *Samuel Pepys's Spanish Plays* (London, 1980),. pp. 85-120; and Cruickshank's 'Calderón and the Spanish Book Trade', in K. and R. Reichenberger, *Bibliographisches Handbuch der Calderón-Forschung*, II (Kassel, 1981), 3-8.

19. Cruickshank, 'Some Aspects of Spanish Book-production'; C. Péligry, 'Les Difficultés de l'édition castillane au XVIIᵉ S. à travers un document de l'époque', *MCV*, 13 (1977), 267-77.

20. Pedro Calderón de la Barca, *En la vida todo es verdad y todo mentira*, edited by D. W. Cruickshank (London, 1971), p. lxv.

21. Calderón, *Primera parte de autos sacramentales* (Madrid, 1677), ¶7ᵛ.

one of the six is definitely by Lope, but a naïve customer might easily assume that several of them were. This particular volume is an octavo, and versions survive with the imprints of both Pedro Madrigal of Madrid and Pedro Craesbeeck of Lisbon. The complete background to the printing of the volume has yet to be investigated.[22]

The problems most likely to be encountered by editors working from printed items are as follows:

1) The unauthorised reprint of a best-seller. Piratical reprints would usually try to pass for variants of an edition already printed. However, no Spanish printer of this period could imitate an earlier edition closely enough to deceive, so the existence of a reprint can always be detected, if copies of the earlier edition survive. Telling which is which may be harder. Example: the VS *Primera parte* of Calderón, '1640'.[23] A better means of disguising the fraud was to use a false imprint; in this way an apparently authorised new edition was produced, which could not be exposed by comparison with the genuine original, and which only an expert in typography could trace back to its printer. Example: the *Tercera parte* of Lope, 'Barcelona, Sebastián de Cormellas, 1612'.[24]

2) The unauthorised 'reproduction' of a best-seller. Printers who wanted to cash in on a successful *parte* without even the cost of reprinting it would bind together twelve *sueltas*, print a set of preliminary leaves, and sell the resulting volume as a slightly variant issue of the genuine original. Example: the complete Vera Tassis edition of Calderón, nine volumes, '1683-1694'.[25]

3) The unauthorised production of the 'first edition' of a *parte*. It was also possible to use existing printed material, whether

22. See A. Castro and H. A. Rennert, *Vida de Lope de Vega (1562-1635)* (Salamanca, 1969), pp. 156-7. Castro and Rennert suggest that the producers of this volume did not set out deliberately to deceive; but if they did not, others certainly did.

23. E. M. Wilson, 'The Two Editions of Calderón's *Primera parte* of 1640', *The Library*, V, 14 (1959), 175-91; D. W. Cruickshank, 'Calderón's *Primera* and *Tercera partes*: The Reprints of "1640" and "1664" ', *The Library*, V, 25 (1970), 105-19.

24. J. Moll, 'La "Tercera parte de las comedias de Lope de Vega y otros auctores", falsificación sevillana', *RABM*, 77 (1974), 619-26.

25. See D. W. Cruickshank and E. M. Wilson, 'A Calderón Collection in Dr. Steevens' Hospital, Dublin', *Long Room*, 9 (1974), 17-27. Something similar happened in the case of Moreto's *Primera* and *Segunda partes* of Valencia, 1676, and perhaps of his *Tercera parte* of Valencia, 1703; further investigation is required, but editions composed of *sueltas* certainly exist, of all three of these *partes*.

sueltas or dismembered fragments of earlier *partes*, to assemble a volume which had not been published before. Such volumes cannot be detected by comparing them with a genuine earlier edition, which does not exist; but as in the previous example, they will give themselves away by their lack of continuous pagination and signatures, or (but not always) lack of typographical consistency. Examples: *Doze comedias nuevas de Lope de Vega Carpio, y otros autores*, 'Barcelona, Gerónimo Margarit, 1630'; *Parte quarenta y dos de comedias de diferentes autores*, 'Zaragoza, Juan de Ybar, 1650'. The second of these has some typographical consistency, although it is composed of *sueltas* and so lacks continuous pagination and signatures.[26] Such a volume might be produced legally, although this will make no practical difference to the bibliographical problems. These arise from the fact that neither the date nor the printer's name on the title-page are to be relied on where the contents are concerned.

4) The *desglosable*, which is a play printed so that it could be fitted into any *parte*, depending on the market. It could even be sold singly as a *suelta*. A *desglosable* was normally fitted into three gatherings of quarto in eights. Since not all plays were equally long, one of the gatherings (generally the last) would vary in size, producing signatures such as these: A^8 B^8 C^2; A^8 B^8 C^8; A^8 B^8 C^{10}. (In all three examples gatherings A and B are regular gatherings of quarto in eights; in the first, gathering C is a half-sheet, two leaves; in the second, two regular sheets; in the third, two and a half sheets.) The play planned for the first place in a volume would be given the first three letters of the alphabet (A-C); that planned for the second place would get D-F, and so on.[27] Continuous pagination was usually supplied, though if it was, it reduced the possibility of switching the *desglosable* from one volume to another; if the pagination were to remain correct, a *desglosable* could be replaced only by another of the same number of leaves. It goes without saying that the preliminaries, with their list of contents, could be printed or reprinted to suit whatever went into the volume;

26. See D. W. Cruickshank, 'The First Edition of *El burlador de Sevilla*', 443-67; and 'The Second Part of *La hija del aire*', in *Golden-Age Studies in Honour of A.A. Parker, BHS*, 61 (1984), 286-94. In fact *Diferentes XLII* may be 'legal', although not all of it was printed by Ybar; two of the *sueltas* were printed by Diego Dormer of Zaragoza.

27. Cruickshank, 'The First Edition of *El burlador de Sevilla*', pp. 444-6.

even so, there are volumes where the contents-list does not match the plays present in the volume, or which combine fragments of true *partes* (not intended to be dismembered) with *desglosables* and with *sueltas*. Examples: Lope's *Parte veynte y cinco*, 'Barcelona, Sebastián de Cormellas, 1631', and his *Parte veinte y siete*, 'Barcelona, Sebastián de Cormellas, 1633'.[28] *Desglosables* were almost never given individual dates and imprints. It cannot be assumed that a *desglosable* was printed at the date and place announced on the title-page of the volume which contains it.

5) The *suelta*. *Comedias* were printed singly in Spain as early as the second decade of the sixteenth century, and continued to be printed in what came to be the traditional *suelta* manner until well into the nineteenth century. The total output of these three centuries was enormous. There may be ten, twenty, even more *surviving* editions of some plays. There are huge numbers with no imprint or date, and not a few in which imprint and date are false, whether by design or accident. In many cases *sueltas* are reprints of earlier editions, whether of *partes* or of other *sueltas*, which have survived. Once they have been identified as such, they can usually be ignored. Occasionally, a *suelta* may be a first edition (Lope's *El castigo sin venganza*, Calderón's *Fieras afemina Amor*) or an only surviving one (*Tan largo me lo fiais*, Rojas Zorrilla's *Lucrecia y Tarquino*).

6) The reissue (only technically illegal). Sometimes, when a volume's sales were declining, publishers would try to revive them by printing fresh preliminaries to make the book seem newer, or perhaps more attractive to a particular local readership. Example: *Parte treinta de diferentes autores*, Zaragoza, 1636; Zaragoza, '1638'; 'Seville, 1638'; Zaragoza, '1639'.[29] At first sight, the discovery that he is dealing with a series of reissues rather than of editions might seem likely to save the editor a great deal of work; in fact he will still have to check all the copies to make certain that

28. For the first, see V. G. Williamsen, 'Lope de Vega: A "Missing" *parte* and Two "Lost" *comedias*', *BCom*, 25 (1973), 42-51; for the second, M. G. Profeti, 'Appunti bibliografici sulla collezione "Diferentes autores"', in *Miscellanea di studi ispanici* (Pisa, 1969-70), pp. 153-5; for both, see Cruickshank, 'The First Edition of *El burlador de Sevilla*', 458-64.

29. Profeti, 'Appunti bibliografici', pp. 162-7; but see in particular V. F. Dixon, 'A Note on *Diferentes 30*', *BHS*, 39 (1962), 92-6. The technical illegality arises from the government's decree (1627) that all printed matter should carry the correct date and imprint.

one of them is not a new edition. Even if this check shows that all the copies are reissues of one edition, every copy may still have its own peculiar press-variants.

If an editor is to fit a printed edition into a diagram of the history of his text, he needs to know when the text was printed and, if possible, by whom. If he does not know this, the text he is editing will be his only source of information about the habits of the compositor/s involved. Once the printer is known, it becomes at least theoretically possible to identify other works set by the same compositor. This in turn makes it easier to discover his habits and preferences, which would give rise to varying degrees of 'editing' in the text being produced.

The editor should begin by collating the *parte* or *suelta* he is working on, i.e. he should note the format and check the number of leaves; doubts should be eliminated by checking more than one copy whenever possible. For example, Calderón's *Primera parte* of Madrid, 1636, collates as: 4°. ¶⁴ A-Z⁸ Aa-Oo⁸. That is, the book is a quarto. It has four preliminary leaves signed with a 'pilcrow' (paragraph mark); they are followed by twenty-three gatherings of quarto in eights, signed A to Z, whereupon the alphabet is repeated as far as O, another fourteen gatherings in eights. Thus the text takes up a total of thirty-seven gatherings of two sheets each (seventy-four), plus one sheet of preliminaries. The title-page actually contains the number '75', a reference to the total number of sheets; this was a common but unfortunately not universal practice at the time. The leaves are foliated, not paginated, and seventy-four sheets (of text, since the preliminaries are not numbered) at four folios each should make 296. In fact some leaves are wrongly numbered, but the number of folios is correct. The editor can be sure that the book was planned as a unit, and is not made up of *sueltas*. The fact that plays begin and end in the midst of gatherings is a sign that the volume could not easily be split up into twelve *desglosables*, and that it was not planned in this fashion. A glance at the type shows that that used in the headings of the individual plays, in their texts (roman and italic) and in the running headlines, is consistent throughout the book. There are no suspicious circumstances about it.[30]

30. There is also evidence of an overlay of compositorial spelling which is consistent throughout the volume, and which can be found in other items produced by María de

When we look for the next edition of this *parte*, we find two editions dated 1640. One of them, said to be printed by the widow of Juan Sánchez 'A costa de Gabriel de Leon mercader de Libros', collates ¶⁴ A-Z⁸ Aa-Oo⁸, and has 296 folios, like the 1636 edition. There is nothing to arouse our suspicions. When we look at the other, with the same printer's name but no mention of Gabriel de León, we see that it has only two preliminary leaves, unsigned, and that the rest collates A-Z⁸ Aa-Ii⁸ KK⁴. The total number of sheets is only 65½, and the text is paginated, not foliated. The '75' which appears on the title-page of the other two editions is not present. If, our suspicions aroused, we investigate what has happened, we find that some preliminary matter has been omitted, and the text compressed. This is not unknown in reprints, and *proves* nothing. The change to pagination, which became popular in the second half of the century, is worth noting. When we look at the type, we at once find discrepancies. The type of gatherings A-L is different from that of M-Ff, while that of Gg-KK is different from both, although closest to that of A-L. Further investigation along typographical lines shows that the book was probably printed about 1670-71 by Lucas Antonio de Bedmar and Melchor Alegre; Alegre printed the middle part, Bedmar the other two, apparently with an interval between them (perhaps the length of time it took Alegre to print M-Ff). The reasons for this division of labour are not clear.[31]

Turning to the next edition of this *parte*, that produced by Vera Tassis in 1685, we again find two versions with the same date. One collates ¶⁸ ¶¶⁶ A-Z⁸ Aa-Ll⁸ Mm⁴, and the text is paginated from 1 to 543 (544 is blank). The typography is reassuringly consistent. When we try to collate the other, we find it impossible: signatures begin afresh with each of the twelve plays; so does the page numbering, when there is any; and the typographical variations are enormous, with differences even between copies. In fact the volume is composed of twelve *sueltas* which are the work of several firms. Different editions of some *sueltas* were used in some of the different copies. External evidence shows that the

Quiñones about this time.
31. See Cruickshank, 'Calderón's *Primera* and *Tercera partes*'.

fraud dates from about 1700-1710, but of course some of the *sueltas* may have been printed much earlier than this. The only sure way to discover their dates is to take them singly and rely on typographical evidence.[32]

It must be emphasized that not only reprints were produced by work-sharing or by making-up. For example, there is evidence that the first edition of *Comedias escogidas XXXIII*, 1670, was begun by Melchor Alegre and completed by José Fernández de Buendía, although naturally the title-page does not furnish this information.[33] In the so-called *Diferentes* series, partes *XLII, XLIII* and *XLIV*, ostensibly printed in Zaragoza between 1650 and 1652, are all composed of *sueltas*, although no earlier editions are known. Not all copies of *XLIV* have identical contents.[34]

We come now to typographical evidence which, as stated above, is the only sure way of discovering the real date and printer of a book with no, or with a false, imprint.

Most printers in Spain gave up using gothic in favour of roman type in the third quarter of the sixteenth century. Thus the great majority of Golden-Age plays, and all of those from Lope de Vega onwards, are printed in roman type. Typographical material has always been expensive, even when labour was cheap. Type-metal alone cost one and a half *reales* per pound, and casting cost four and a half *reales* per 1000 pieces. A minimally useful fount of pica (about twelve points today, and the size most frequently used for plays in the seventeenth century) would weigh upwards of 200 pounds and involve 50,000 or so pieces, at a cost of rather more than 500 *reales*; if constantly used, it might not last a year. A set of matrices with a type-mould, which would enable a properly trained printer to cast his own type, was likely to cost much more than 1000 *reales* for a text-type, to which had to be added over 300 *reales* for a usable amount of metal. Once purchased, the metal would last indefinitely, but matrices and moulds eventually wore out. In any case, both matrices and skilled typefounders were scarce in Spain.

32. See Cruickshank and Wilson, 'A Calderón Collection'.
33. Cruickshank, 'Calderón's *Primera* and *Tercera partes*', 152, 156-7.
34. See Profeti, 'Appunti bibliografici', pp. 175-80, for descriptions of *Diferentes XLII, XLIII* and *XLIV*; and p. 179 for the variant contents of *XLIV*.

Given the parlous state of the Spanish printing industry, few printers could contemplate such major capital outlays often enough to maintain high standards. Their typographical material was generally worn, damaged, adulterated and improvised. They got type from where they could; seldom concerned to get the best, they got instead what was most readily available. The result is that in much of the Golden Age, the typographical material of each printer was relatively distinct.

During the period in question, Spain's chief sources of type were France, the Low Countries and Italy. Type deriving from the French designers, Garamont, Granjon and Haultin, was everywhere common, and predominant in Madrid. Printers in the Seville area enjoyed the benefits of shipping links with the Netherlands, and so had a higher proportion of type deriving from the Flemish punchcutters François Guyot, Ameet Tavernier and Hendrik van den Keere; after 1648 they also got type from Dutch foundries, some of it Dutch (e.g. Christoffel van Dijk), some of it of German origin (e.g. Voskens of Hamburg and Berner of Frankfurt). In the kingdom of Aragón there was less Flemish, Dutch or German type, at least during the seventeenth century. The type there was largely French, with some Italian, e.g. from the Vatican foundry.

Apart from providing evidence about the whereabouts of a book's printing, type also helps with dating. In some cases we know when a design was produced; in others we know when it arrived in Spain. The 13mm capitals of the Vatican foundry were first used in Italy in 1612-13 and in Spain about 1619; Spanish books which appear to use them before 1619 (and certainly before 1612-13) should be regarded with suspicion. Similarly, three sets of capitals were cut in Madrid about 1685 by one Pedro Disses.[35] Books which use them before this date are frauds; for example, the fake Vera Tassis versions of Calderón's *Sexta* and *Séptima partes* (1683) could be rejected for this reason alone.

The easiest method of identifying the date and printer of a

35. D.W. Cruickshank, 'The Types of Pedro Disses', *Journal of the Printing Historical Society*, 17 (1982-83), 72-91. Evidence from one document and from numerous printed books reveals that while Disses may have begun work on his capitals as early as 1683, they were not ready for use until the summer and autumn of 1685.

suspect or imprintless item is to draw up a list of its typographical material, from the largest roman to the smallest, the largest to the smallest italic, and finally of the ornaments, whether they are made of metal or of wood (it will not always be possible to distinguish wood from metal; but if an apparently identical ornament is used more than once in the same forme, then it will almost certainly be metal). If the design can be identified from the various facsimiles of old founders' specimens, so much the better: this may provide information about dates and places, as suggested above.[36] If a typeface or ornament cannot be identified in this way, the investigator will need to obtain a photocopy of it for comparison. He must then look for books which use the same typographical material in circumstances which give rise to no suspicion. This is the hardest part of the process, particularly for someone with no access to large numbers of old books. If the investigator has no evidence to help him limit the initial scope of his search, the task may be impossible. It is true to say, however, that any intelligent and observant person who examines the type of a sizable number of old books will become reasonably good at guessing when an undated one was printed, and eventually where it was printed. Besides, the increasing availability of facsimiles and microfilm collections of old books makes it less and less necessary to consult the originals.[37]

There will be many cases when it will not be necessary to establish exactly when an edition was printed, and by whom; that is, a guess such as 'Madrid, 1660-1680?' will often be enough to establish the chronological relationship of that edition to others, a relationship which textual evidence will usually confirm. Only in

36. The most helpful type specimens for the Hispanist are: *Type Specimen Facsimiles*, edited by John Dreyfus, 2 volumes (London, 1963-72); H.D.L. Vervliet, *Sixteenth-century Printing Types of the Low Countries* (Amsterdam, 1968); *The Type Specimen of the Vatican Press 1628*, edited by H.D.L. Vervliet (Amsterdam, 1967); *The Type Specimen of Delacolonge*, edited by Harry Carter (Amsterdam, 1969); *The Type-specimens of Claude Lamesle*, edited by A.F. Johnson (Amsterdam, 1965).

37. Facsimiles of some of the earliest Golden-Age plays have existed for many years, e.g. Encina's *Cancionero* of 1496 (1928), Lucas Fernández's *Farsas y églogas* of 1514 (1929), Torres Naharro's *Propalladia* of 1517 (1936), Diego Sánchez de Badajoz's *Recopilación en metro* of 1554 (1929), Gil Vicente's *Copilaçam de todalas obras* of 1562 (1928) and the *Autos, comedias y farsas de la Biblioteca Nacional* (1962). The most ambitious facsimile of a late dramatist is *The comedias of Calderón* (1973), but publishers such as Puvill of Barcelona are gradually making available more and more old Spanish printing in facsimile or microfiche.

cases when such an edition is to be used to establish the text will it be necessary to investigate further the circumstances of its printing.

Some rules for the dating of imprintless *sueltas* were set out by Edward M. Wilson in 1973.[38] Since they have been refined and added to in the past decade, they will bear repeating here. Further research will certainly produce more refinements.

1) *Format.* Quarto in eights became the standard format for *partes* and for *sueltas* during the second decade of the seventeenth century; for *partes* it remained so, with rare late exceptions such as the Apontes edition of Calderón. *Sueltas*, on the other hand, switched from quarto in eights to quarto in fours during the years 1650 to 1670. Further research is desirable, but a *suelta* in eights will probably be early, perhaps before 1650, while one in fours will probably be later, perhaps after 1670.

2) *Title-pages.* As a rule, *sueltas* had individual title-pages only in the late sixteenth and early seventeenth centuries, but a few *sueltas* were given title-pages both earlier and later than this. Some of the later ones may be special editions linked to first performances (like Calderón's *Fieras afemina Amor*).

3) *Serial numbers.* *Sueltas* began to have serial numbers about 1700. Some valuable research has been done on these numbers; it has been shown, for example, that neither they nor dates are entirely to be trusted. Some reprints were given the old serial number and a new date; others reprinted the date along with the rest, and can be identified only by type and paper.[39]

4) *Spelling and punctuation.* During the period when *sueltas* were being printed, there was a gradual but uneven progression towards modern spelling and punctuation. The investigator will soon get used to noticing the changes, although their uneven nature makes them difficult to use for precise dating. Printers in Seville, with

---

38. E.M. Wilson, '*Comedias sueltas*—a Bibliographical Problem', in *The comedias of Calderón*, I, 211-19.

39. For serial numbers, see J. Moll, 'Las nueve partes de Calderón editadas en comedias sueltas (Barcelona, 1763-1767)', *BRAE*, 51 (1971), 259-304, and 'La serie numerada de comedias de la imprenta de los Orga', *RABM*, 75 (1968-72), 365-456; W.T. McCready, 'Las comedias sueltas de la casa de Orga', in *Homenaje a William L. Fichter* (Madrid, 1971), 515-24; A.J.C. Bainton, 'The *comedias sueltas* of Antonio Sanz', *TCBS*, VII, 2 (1978), 248-54.

their access to the new Dutch designs, began using J and U (for consonantal I and vocalic V) in the 1670s; this change did not become widespread in Madrid printing until the 1690s. The adoption of short s and inverted punctuation (¿¡) belongs to the second half of the eighteenth century, although it varies from printer to printer; further research is needed. The use of :: or ::: or ::- for modern three points (...) had a brief vogue in the mid eighteenth century. A lot of research remains to be done on ordinary spelling habits, e.g. on when the printers stopped using initial 'y' for 'i' or 'ç' for 'z'.

5) *Size and design of type.* Plays were usually printed in pica (*lectura* or *cícero*) in the seventeenth century; the size of body varied from 79 to 89mm per twenty lines. The larger bodies are particularly associated with Madrid founders in the second half of the century. Naturally Madrid printers used the type of Madrid founders, but Madrid type was used further afield as well—sometimes even in Seville. Seville printers were printing plays with text-types of 65-69mm/20 lines (long primer, *entredós*) in the 1670s, but sizes in the 70-79mm range (small pica, *lectura chica*) are associated with the very end of the seventeenth and with the eighteenth century. The practice of printing some gatherings—usually the last one—of *sueltas* in smaller type in order to fit them more neatly into a whole number of sheets seems to have begun at the end of the seventeenth century. This was just when small pica was coming into regular use (usually pica and small pica are the two faces involved). It should not be confused with the practice of using two different founts of pica in one play, a practice which almost certainly points to two compositors. Measurement of the body-size will prevent confusion. Apart from text-types, titling types can also help in dating, as already pointed out. There was a constant influx of new titling types into Spanish printing during the Golden Age. In some cases, the date of production of the original designs is known; in others, the date of their introduction into Spain has been deduced. In many cases only the experience of looking at dated books will allow the investigator to become adept at guessing the dates of undated items.[40]

---

40. On type, see G.T. Tanselle, 'The Identification of Type Faces in Bibliographical Description', *PBSA*, 60 (1966), 185-202. For the method of measuring type, see Gaskell, *A New Introduction*, pp. 13-14; for some useful terminology, see the same author's 'A Nomenclature for the Letter-forms of Roman Type', *The Library*, V, 29 (1974) 42-51.

6) *Paper*. Too little research has been done on Spanish paper, and in particular on that of the seventeenth and eighteenth centuries. The investigator who hopes to use paper as evidence in dating will have to gather much of the basic information himself. The task will be complicated by the fact that *sueltas* were frequently printed on poor paper, which the manufacturers did not always watermark; and by the fact that not all watermarks can be trusted, since a lot of imported paper bearing the Genoese mark was really produced in Holland. However, the one serious attempt to date *sueltas* from paper shows that some of the difficulties can be surmounted, and that evidence from paper, if applied in the proper circumstances, can be valuable.[41]

*   *   *   *   *

After this long preliminary, we may now return to the consideration of the seven different parts of the author's task, as set down at the beginning.

1   *Tracing surviving editions and investigating relationships between them*

In recent years two major bibliographies of Spanish Golden-Age dramatists have appeared: M.G. Profeti's *Per una bibliografia di Juan Pérez de Montalbán*, and the *Calderón-Handbuch* of K. and R. Reichenberger.[42] In theory these list all the known

---

41. See B. Scarfe, 'A Role for Watermarks in Bibliographical Description', *Bulletin of the Bibliographical Society of Australia and New Zealand*, 12 (1978), 85-101. The standard textbooks on watermarks (but which are unlikely to be of much help to Hispanists) include C. Briquet, *Les Filigranes* (Paris, 1907, and Amsterdam, 1968); F. de Bofarull y Sans, *Los animales en las marcas de papel* (Barcelona, 1910 and, in English, Hilversum, 1959); W.A. Churchill, *Watermarks in Paper in the XVIIth and XVIIIth Centuries* (Amsterdam, 1935 and 1967); E. Heawood, *Watermarks Mainly of the XVIIth and XVIIIth Centuries* (Hilversum, 1950, and Amsterdam, 1970). See also Péligry, 'Les difficultés de l'édition castillane', 272-5.

42. The first was published in Verona in 1976; the second will consist of three volumes, of which two have been published (Kassel, 1979, 1981). No other major author has been treated so comprehensively. *Lopistas* must make do with the 'Bibliografía de las obras dramáticas de Lope de Vega' in Castro and Rennert, *Vida de Lope de Vega*, pp. 431-503, or with R.L. Grismer's *Bibliography of Lope de Vega*, 2 volumes (Minneapolis, 1965); S.G. Morley and C. Bruerton, *The Chronology of Lope de Vega's comedias* (London & New York, 1940; revised Spanish edition, Madrid, 1968), though not a bibliography, is always helpful. There are bibliographies for many other authors, and C.A. de la Barrera's *Catálogo bibliográfico y biográfico del teatro antiguo español* (Madrid, 1860 and London, 1968) is still worth consulting.

editions of the work of the authors concerned, and the whereabouts of all known copies of the earliest editions. In practice, of course, a bibliography is almost by definition incomplete, but these two works are indispensable starting-points for any textual study of Pérez de Montalbán or Calderón. There exist various other bibliographies of Spanish Golden-Age dramatic literature, some dealing with authors, some with particular collections, with individual volumes or with particular plays. Of special usefulness are the various catalogues of *comedias sueltas* which have appeared in the course of the last half-century.[43] Not all libraries, especially in Spain itself, have published catalogues, however, and editors must be ready to contemplate writing to and even visiting some of them to ascertain what their holdings are.

When the editor has completed a list of all known early editions of his play, he must arrange them in a *stemma*, i.e. in a family tree. Mere chronology, once it has been established in accordance with the information given above, will provide a starting-point, but it should be confirmed from textual evidence. For example, close examination of any early edition of a play will reveal misprints and obvious errors, no matter how carefully it was produced. When such an edition was reprinted, the compositor would automatically correct obvious errors. Sometimes he would miscorrect an error, and as compensation for his successful corrections, he would introduce fresh errors. All this will seem very clear when the precedence of the one text over the other is certain or nearly so. When it is not, the matter is quite different. It is sometimes very hard to determine, from textual variants alone, which of two closely-related prints of a play is the earlier. If there is

43. P.P. Rogers, *The Spanish Drama Collection in the Oberlin College Library—A Descriptive Catalogue* (Oberlin, 1940); J.A. Molinaro, J.H. Parker and E. Rugg, *A Bibliography of comedias sueltas in the University of Toronto Library* (Toronto, 1959); B.B. Ashcom, *A Descriptive Catalogue of the Spanish comedias sueltas in the Wayne State University Library and the Private Library of Professor B.B. Ashcom* (Detroit, 1965); W.A. McKnight and M.B. Jones, *A Catalogue of the comedias sueltas in the Library of the University of North Carolina* (Chapel Hill, 1965); J. Moll, *Catálogo de comedias sueltas conservadas en la Biblioteca de la Real Academia Española* (Madrid, 1966); A.J.C. Bainton, *Comedias sueltas in Cambridge University Library: A Descriptive Catalogue* (Cambridge, 1977); M.V. Boyer, *The Texas Collection of comedias sueltas: A Descriptive Bibliography* (Boston, 1978); E.M. Wilson and D.W. Cruickshank, *Samuel Pepys's Spanish Plays* (London, 1980); H.E. Bergman and Szilvia E. Szmuk, *A Catalogue of comedias sueltas in New York Public Library*, 2 volumes (London, 1980-81). Karl C. Gregg, *An Index to the Spanish Theatre Collection in the London Library* (Charlottesville, 1984).

a reasonable interval between them, older fashions in spelling, punctuation and capitalisation will point (though not infallibly) to the earlier. If the practice of the author himself is well documented in these areas, one can usually assume that successive editions will diverge more and more from it. If one of the editions omits anything which is present in the other, the more complete version is likely to be the earlier, since compositors' corrections did not as a rule extend to making good omissions. None of these methods is entirely reliable. It may be said, though, that if an editor is faced with a pair of texts (say, two *sueltas*) so similar that he cannot tell which was printed from which, he should not worry, since it cannot be very important. In most cases such a pair of editions will occur well down the stemma, where they can have no bearing on a definitive text; if they happen to constitute the first and second editions of the play, it will hardly matter which is chosen as the copy-text: any differences significant enough to be of importance in a definitive edition will provide evidence of precedence.

To a certain extent, the process of investigating relationships between texts can be reduced to a formula. The example most readily available to readers of English is Sir W.W. Greg's *Calculus of Variants* (1927), which W.F. Hunter has shown how to adapt for Spanish dramatic texts.[44] Greg shows how to interpret the evidence of different groups of variants, and is well worth any editor's trouble to read. However, his method was intended to be used, and is most useful when dealing with manuscripts, such as we find among Calderón's *autos*. Undated manuscripts can rarely be dated with any precision, unlike a printed edition; every manuscript is unique, and since unique items are easily lost, we rarely find an example of manuscript transmission which has no manuscripts missing. Printed editions disappear less frequently, and since most are dated or datable, much of the task of establishing relationships can be done by simple chronology, without recourse to formulae. Any editor who feels apprehensive should examine the introductions of a few reliable editions, or read some of the number of appropriate textual studies. The best of

---

44. W.F. Hunter, 'Métodos de crítica textual', in *Hacia Calderón*, edited by H. Flasche (Berlin, 1970), 13-28; see also V. Dearing, *Methods of Textual Editing* (Los Angeles, 1962).

these give examples of how progressive corruption and/or correction can be detected in successive versions or editions.[45]

An editor with access to a computer will be able to do the more mechanical parts of his task with greater speed and accuracy. Computers have already been used to compare different versions of a text to find variants. The versions are typed into the computer, which is programmed to produce a variant-list; if the typist is guilty of errors or omissions, these will be recorded as variants, and the faults can be put right by checking the originals. Only if the same error is repeated in the typing of the different versions will difficulties occur, but even this can be eliminated by proper checking. Nowadays, however, it is not necessary to type the texts: some computers can read print. Furthermore, computer programmes can be written to do the more mechanical parts of classifying variants according to Greg's *Calculus*. In the last resort the editor will still have to use his own judgement to assess the priority of one text over others, but he will have saved a good deal of time.[46]

2 *Identifying versions of the text which must have existed but which are lost*

A version of a text which must have existed but now does not is called 'inferential' (because its existence can be inferred). The commonest inferential version which an editor will encounter is the author's original. There may sometimes have been cases of composition by dictation, but for practical purposes we can invariably assume, with no evidence but a printed edition, that a holographic original once existed. Other inferential texts will require more evidence. Dates, places or other features of the

---

45. See, for example, E.M. Wilson's 'Notes on the Text of *A secreto agravio secreta venganza'*, *BHS*, 35 (1958), 72-82; 'The Text of Calderón's *La púrpura de la rosa'*, *MLR*, 54 (1959), 29-44; and 'La edición príncipe de *Fieras afemina amor* de don Pedro Calderón de la Barca', *RBAM*, 24 (1960, for 1955), 7-28.

46. See H. Love, 'The Computer and Literary Editing: Achievements and Prospects', in *The Computer in Literary and Linguistic Research*, edited by R.A. Wisbey (Cambridge, 1971), pp. 47-56; for a more recent (and more technical) review, see W. Ott, 'A Text Processing System for the Preparation of Critical Editions', *Computers and the Humanities*, 13 (1979), 29-35; for a practical example, see R.L. Widmann, 'The Computer in Historical Collation: Use of the IBM 360/75 in Collating Multiple Editions of *A Midsummer Night's Dream'*, in *The Computer in Literary and Linguistic Research*, pp. 57-63.

wording of a book's preliminaries may lead us to suppose that the earliest known edition is not the first. This is true of Lope's *Tercera parte*, which probably appeared first in 1611, in Valencia.[47] Alternatively, an edition of, say, 1650 may vary so much from one of 1620 that an editor may conclude that another intervened. These are risky arguments, however; generations of editors have created hundreds of ghosts (editions which never existed) by misuse of them, the most notorious being the '1604' *Don Quixote*.

A more trustworthy method of identifying inferential versions is from textual evidence. Consider a text of which two editions appeared more or less simultaneously in different places. They vary too much to have been printed one from the other without revision; each has lines not present in the other, but yet they share errors or areas of textual confusion, such as an author is not likely to have produced. We can infer a common ancestor which contained these errors or confusions, and which was therefore not the author's original. We can infer also, as usual, the existence of a version which *was* in the author's hand. The stemma would look like this:

This is the stemma of *La vida es sueño*, where *O is Calderón's original, *C the inferential common ancestor, QCL the Madrid edition and Z the Zaragoza one, both of 1636. The stemma is complicated by Calderón's revision, prior to the existence of QCL, but after that of *C, of what he wrote in *O. (That is, his original version reached Z via *C, his revised version reached QCL via *C.) Zaragoza is far from Madrid, so it seems unreasonable to suppose that *C served as printer's copy in Zaragoza, found its way back to Madrid to be revised, then served as printer's copy for QCL; it is also unreasonable since there is some evidence that both books

47. See Caroline Monahan, 'The Transmission of the Text of Luis Vélez' *Los hijos de la Barbuda*', *The Library*, V, 33 (1978), 153-7, especially the stemma on p. 156.

were being set at the same time. So we can infer another version; presumably it intervened between *C and Z or between *C and QCL. We cannot say which, and cannot place it in the stemma.

Another means of detecting inferential versions is through accidentals, mainly spelling. If we had a *parte* of twelve authentic *comedias* by one author, of which one betrayed spelling peculiarities not found in the others, we could reasonably conclude that the play had not been set from the author's original— reasonably, that is, once we had eliminated the possibility that that play had been set by a different compositor.

Detecting inferential versions of a text is a necessary part of drawing up a stemma: it will enable the editor not merely to discover which surviving version of his text is nearest to the original, but *how* near it is. This is important, since the kind of edition produced, and the extent of the editor's intervention, will to some extent depend upon it. It may be said, as a general rule, that the nearer an editor's basic text is to the original, the less he will tamper with it.

3 *Identifying the version to be used as the basis for the edition*
Sometimes a stemma will turn out to be a simple line: edition 2 produced from 1, 3 from 2, 4 from 3, and so on. If that is so, edition 1 will provide the basis, *even if subsequent editions have been revised or corrected.* This is an important principle, with all the authority of Greg and McKerrow behind it: 'in all normal cases of correction or revision the original edition should still be taken as the copy-text'.[48] 'Normal cases' means those where revision or correction are carried out by marking-up a copy of the first edition and giving it to the printer as copy for the second. 'Abnormal' cases might involve those in which the author re-transcribed the work as he revised it, giving the new autograph manuscript to the printer. But how to tell the normal from the abnormal? How to choose between two independent editions of ostensibly equal weight, as in the stemma illustrated above? For that matter, how can one distinguish an authentic authorial revision from an unauthorised and unauthoritative compositorial alteration?

48. W.W. Greg, 'The Rationale of Copy-text', *SB*, 3 (1950-51), 33.

No editor should set out to prepare an edition of any author without first having read a great deal of the work of that author and his contemporaries. (If the author wrote only one play, the editor must make do with the contemporaries, although this will be a poor substitute.) An editor who is thoroughly familiar with his author will often be able to reject some 'corrections' as merely compositorial, while accepting others as authentic. This may not sound very scientific, but it can be made more so by quoting chapter and verse for other examples, found in other works by the author, to support the authenticity of words, metaphors, turns of phrase and even verse-forms.[49] The growing number of concordances, metrical studies and linguistic analyses being produced for Golden-Age authors will greatly simplify this operation.

All this involves the substantives of a text. Of equal importance are the accidentals: spelling, punctuation, capitalisation, accentuation, lineation. Nowadays we have rules governing such matters. The rules are relatively strict, but they allow for some individual preferences in the use of some signs of punctuation, some spellings (-ise versus -ize, etc.), and permit us to detect, if only on a global scale, regional variations (labor, labour, theater, theatre, etc.). To the untutored reader, written Spanish of the Golden Age may seem to have had no such rules, but this is false: the rules were there, but they were less strict, and thus gave a wider scope to individual preferences. To complicate matters further, there was a considerable variation between the rules as applied to printed Spanish and as applied to the handwritten language (this variation is still with us, in that we expect the printed language to adhere more closely to the rules, and, where the rules are flexible, to be consistent: hence the need for journals to provide contributors with style-sheets). Spanish writing-masters, if they did not provide specific recommendations regarding spelling, punctuation and capitalisation, would advise their pupils to imitate the usage of

---

49. For example, a variant *quintilla* whose rhyme-scheme differed from the consistent ababa of all the others in a passage helped Dr. Monahan to reject one possible copy-text in favour of another: 'The Transmission of the Text of Luis Vélez'...', 157.

good compositors.[50] It is clear, however, that many authors, even when they wrote with publication in mind, paid scant attention to such advice; they expected the printers to be their sub-editors, to be final arbiters of what was correct.[51] In practice, the printers, working as they were within a flexible set of rules, and from manuscript material written according to even more flexible rules, never managed to impose an absolute degree of consistency. For example, at least part of Calderón's *Quarta parte* was set by two compositors, who tended to do two pages each of every four-page forme. They are most easily distinguished by their spelling of the name Deidamia, a character in *El monstruo de los jardines*, the third play: one preferred *Deidamia*, the other *Deydamia*. The *Deydamia* compositor also preferred the spellings *boluer* and *fè*, his companion *bolver* and *fee*. When the *parte* was reprinted in 1674, corrections and alterations meant that it did not follow the old edition on a page-for-page basis. Nevertheless, the new compositor or compositors were influenced by the spelling of their copy, even changing from *Deidamia* to *Deydamia* in mid page. Given the tendency exemplified by this case, editors should always consider the possibility that variant spellings in a given edition may not point to two or more compositors in that edition, but may derive from an earlier edition, or from two or more scribes (or even authors) in a manuscript.

Both Lope de Vega and Calderón have left large amounts of autograph material, covering the greater part of their careers. The investigator has the wherewithal, if he wishes, to discover the preferences of these two authors with regard to accidentals at almost any stage of their writing lives.[52] Indeed, it would be possible,

50. For example: 'Para enesto no hay mejor, que recorrer alos estampadores, a quien principalmente el officio y cargo de bien apuntar la escriptura esta encomẽdado': Juan de Yciar, *Arte subtilissima, por la qual se enseña a escreuir perfactamente*, a facsimile of the 1550 edition, prepared by Evelyn Shuckburgh and Reynolds Stone (Oxford, 1960), L3ᵛ. Or consider the title of Francisco Tomás de Cerdaña's booklet: *Breve tratado de orthographia latina, y castellana, sacada del estilo de buenos autores latinos y castellanos, y del uso de buenos tipografos* (Valencia, 1645).

51. Among the few authors who imposed their own spelling were Gonzalo Correas, whose *Ortografía kastellana* appeared in 1630 with specially-cut letters, and Fernando de Herrera, whose modest reforms can be seen in his works printed in Seville from 1572 to 1592.

52. Many photographs and facsimiles have been published of the manuscripts of Lope and Calderón, although they represent only a fraction of the material available. It must be remembered that authors' habits tended to change over the years. See Cruickshank, 'Calderón's Handwriting', *MLR*, 65 (1970), 65-77.

within certain limits, to reconstruct the appearance of a word or phrase written by Lope or Calderón at most stages of their careers. For most other authors this will be harder, sometimes impossible; but it is important that an editor should know, in so far as he can, what the autograph manuscript of his author's play would have looked like. The reason for this is that personal peculiarities of handwriting, together with personal preferences in spelling and other accidentals, would combine to produce a unique document. If these peculiarities and personal preferences were such as to cause difficulties in decipherment and therefore, in some cases, errors, the errors in their turn might be peculiar to one author or, at least, characteristic of him. Once an editor is aware of the way in which such characteristic errors were made, then he stands a chance of reversing them with some degree of confidence.[53]

As pointed out above, successive copyings or printings tended to dilute the accidentals of the author's original. As a general rule, if an author's accidentals are very eccentric, and these eccentricities are largely preserved in a printed edition, that edition is unlikely to be far removed from the author's original. Naturally, the eccentricities which have the best rate of survival are those involving rare words or proper names: scribes and compositors, unsure of the 'correct' spelling of a rare word or of the identity of a proper name, tended to preserve the spellings they found.[54]

The extent to which compositors impose their own style upon their copy will, of course, vary. This is one of the ways in which compositors can be identified. The painstaking researches

---

53. For some examples, see Cruickshank, 'Some Uses of Palaeographic and Orthographical Evidence in comedia Editing', BCom, 24 (1973), 40-5.

54. Thus Calderonian spellings 'edna' and 'adlante' (for Etna and Atlante, found in his autograph manuscripts over a lengthy period) are sometimes preserved in early printed editions. In the Tercera parte text of En la vida todo es verdad y todo mentira, a press-correction altered the 'standard' spelling 'decidido' to the more eccentric 'dicidido'. This suggests that the compositor's copy had 'dicidido', a deduction which is supported by the fact that in the autograph manuscript, which survives, Calderón wrote 'dicidido'. In the same volume, however, another press-correction altered 'O tu, Belcro, dios' to 'O tu, Belero, dios'. Another source reveals that no proper name was intended, but the adjective 'velero'. Our knowledge of Calderón's spelling indicates that he would have written this word with a 'v'; he must have intended to say 'O tú, velero dios' (referring to Cupid). The partial correction of the parte suggests tha the compositor's copy was not Calderón's original: see his Tercera parte de comedias (Madrid, 1664), fol. 18^r, col. 1, line 25; and fol. 210^r, col. 2, line 33.

of Dr. R.M. Flores on the text of *Don Quixote* have shown that the whole printed page, including type and the spaces between, is of statistical value in this respect. Compositors had differing preferences in spelling, capitalisation, punctuation, accents, abbreviations, spaces (particularly in association with marks of punctuation); the width of the type-measure, the number of lines per page, the positioning of signatures and catchwords: all these are variants which can provide information about compositors.[55] If, as sometimes happened, different compositors set their type from different cases, the condition of the type might vary, as might the availability and even the design of different sorts; the recurrence of damaged and identifiable individual sorts, and the intervals at which they recur, can also provide information about how a book was set up.[56]

The availability of certain sorts of type is particularly connected with plays. Plays generally contain a high proportion of capital letters (because of the many short speeches and proper names), as well as of queries and exclamation marks. More than the usual amount of italic type was needed for speakers' names and stage directions. Compositors tended to run short of certain sorts (especially queries and italic capitals). Instead they used roman capitals and improvised queries by turning semi-colons upside-down. It will often be possible to discover the order in which pages were set, or to guess at the amount of type available, by noticing at what point the compositor began to show signs of running out of some sorts. Unfortunately, investigations of this kind will be complicated by the fact that composition was sometimes held up while the compositor waited for the pressmen to print an earlier forme which he could then distribute to get fresh type.[57]

The purpose of all this kind of investigation is to help identify the editor's basic text, and the extent of the compositor's 'editorial' intervention in the printing of it. It will also reveal

55. R.M. Flores, *The Compositors of the First and Second Madrid Editions of Don Quixote, Part I* (London, 1975); and 'The Compositors of the First Edition of *Don Quixote*, Part II', *JHP*, 6 (1981), 3-44.

56. The classic example of this kind of scholarship is C. Hinman's *The Printing and Proof-reading of the First Folio of Shakespeare* (Oxford, 1963).

57. Cf. T.L. Berger, 'The Printing of *Henry V*, Q1', *The Library*, VI, 1 (1979), 118-20, 125.

textual problems, ranging from obvious errors and omissions to obscure passages which may be made to yield sense. In the majority of cases the editor will have other editions to which he can turn for help in solving the problems. There is no point, however, in adopting suggestions from other editions without knowing how much authority they have. This brings us to section four.

4 *Identifying other versions which may be used to correct the copy-text*

If the stemma has been drawn up correctly, it will often be immediately obvious which versions of the text are most likely to be of use in correcting errors in the basic text. Versions which derive directly from the basic text cannot have readings with more authority than it has, unless they have been corrected by the author or by someone with access to another version. (This does not mean that directly-derived versions are of no use; the attempted corrections of another editor, even if they have no authority but his own, can often help to resolve, or at least to cast new light on, textual cruces or editorial problems.) The most helpful versions will be those which are not far removed from the author's original, but of which the line of descent diverges from that of the basic text. This can be illustrated with reference to the stemma of *La vida es sueño*:

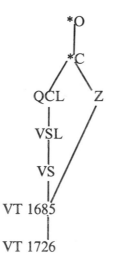

The stemma has already been discussed down to QCL and Z. VSL is a relatively close reprint of QCL, reproducing some errors, correcting others, introducing a few errors of its own.[58] There is no evidence of an authoritative attempt to correct the text, although the nominal editor, Calderón's brother José, was alive in 1640. As we have seen, VS was really produced about 1670, when Calderón at least was still alive. It was printed from VSL, since it makes some errors which can derive only from VSL, but it has more ambitious corrections than the latter; these *may* be Calderonian.[59] The first Vera Tassis edition of 1685 was printed from VS, but there is evidence that Vera also used Z; apparently he had no other source.[60] Finally, the second Vera Tassis edition was produced in 1726. The date of Vera's death is not known, but he was almost certainly dead by then. There is no sign of any serious attempt at correction in the reprint.

The 1726 edition, for practical purposes, is of no use to an editor. The 1685 edition, although it shows how Vera tried to produce correct texts, has no more authority than the still extant texts from which it derives. We may consult Vera to see how he tackled an error shared by QCL and Z; we may even adopt his suggestion; but we must remember that there is no proof that it is anything but his suggestion.

The stemma reveals that the only authoritative texts are QCL and Z, which, because they have a collateral relationship, offer a real hope of reconstructing the lost *C. The few possibly authentic corrections in VS are not shown in the stemma because of the doubts about their origin. In any case they are too few to be very significant.

58. For example, in line 1601, VSL retains QCL's error 'las ruinas'; in 1286, VSL corrects QCL's 'vecellas' to 'vencellas'; but in 1480 omits QCL's 'con' in error.

59. In 1480, VS restores the 'con' omitted by VSL; in 1643, VS changes VSL's wrong 'hacerle' to 'hacerlo', although QCL reads 'hacerse' (this shows that VS was not corrected with reference to QCL, but it does not prove that Calderón did *not* make the correction; he could hardly have recalled in 1670 what he had written in 1635); in 1697 VS alters VSL's 'tu' (which makes sense) to 'tan', the kind of 'improvement' that authors often make; in 2747, VS corrects VSL's meaningless 'de vna' to 'Dafne'.

60. See A.E. Sloman's edition (Manchester, 1961), pp. xxxvi-xxxvii; a good example is lines 700-1, where QCL reads 'En este misero, en este / mortal Planeta, ò signo'. Line 701 is short, and VT reads 'En aqueste, pues, del Sol / ya frenesi, ò ya delirio'. This is Z's reading, apart from 'delito' for 'delirio', which must be VT's own change. All line-references are to Sloman's edition.

As stated earlier, QCL represents a revision of the text, Z the original version. If we are to adhere strictly to the recommendations made by Greg with regard to the editing of revised texts, our procedure ought to be to take Z as our basis and revise it from QCL. In fact no editor has ever done this; many have ignored Z, and those who have used it have taken QCL as the basic text, adopting selected readings from Z. This is not entirely satisfactory; the business of knowing when to correct a basic text by adopting a reading from another one is such an important part of editing that it is best to adhere, as far as possible, to a good set of principles. Greg offered a set of principles for the guidance of authors in precisely this kind of case. When the fact of revision is established, he said,

> an editor should in every case of variation ask himself (1) whether the original reading is one that can reasonably be attributed to the author, and (2) whether the later reading is one that the author can reasonably be supposed to have substituted for the former. If the answer to the first question is negative, then the later reading should be accepted as at least possibly an authoritative correction (unless, of course, it is itself incredible). If the answer to (1) is affirmative and the answer to (2) is negative, the original reading should be retained. If the answers to both questions are affirmative, then the later reading should be presumed to be due to revision and admitted into the text, whether the editor considers it an improvement or not.

It must not be thought, however, that adherence to such principles will make the whole process automatic and release the editor from the need to think: 'No juggling with copy-text will relieve him of the duty and necessity of exercising his own judgement'.[61]

A few cruces from *La vida es sueño* will serve as examples. In lines 1600-2, QCL has:

> Yo vi entre piedras finas
> de la docta Academia de sus ruinas
> preferir el diamante,...

---

61. Greg, 'The Rationale of Copy-text', 32, 34.

This is pretty meaningless. Where QCL reads 'sus ruinas', Z reads 'las minas'. If we take Z as our basis, we should conclude (1) that the original reading (las minas) can reasonably be attributed to Calderón and (2) that the later reading (sus ruinas) is not one that can reasonably be supposed to have been substituted for the former. The Z reading is therefore retained, on the assumption that 'preferir' here means 'to take precedence', a sense that can be supported from other passages in the play. (In practice modern editors who have taken QCL as their basis, but who have consulted Z, have adopted Z's reading. This illustrates an important editorial maxim: good sense can make up for faulty principles. Contrariwise, even sound principles will not compensate for a lack of good sense. Best of all is to have sound principles and to apply them sensibly.) In line 448, we find that in Z Clotaldo says that honour

es de materia tan fragil

while QCL reads 'facil' for 'fragil'. At first sight this example appears to be like the previous one, in which QCL makes nonsense of a good Z reading. However, a glance at the *Diccionario de Autoridades* reveals that 'fácil' can also mean 'frágil', while in *La cisma de Ingalaterra* we can find a description of a moth flying round a light

hasta que deja
en monumento fácil abrasadas
las alas de color tornasoladas.   (410-12)

This is really a case in which the answer to both Greg's questions is affirmative, so we must conclude that QCL's reading is Calderón's own revision. There is a similar case in line 631, where QCL reads

y que campean los signos

while Z offers 'iluminan' for 'campean'. 'Campear' means 'to light up' here; it is recorded in Covarrubias's *Tesoro*, and Calderón's use of it is confirmed by a glance at the Hamburg concordance of his *autos*, which records five occurrences.

As it happens, if we knew nothing of the relationshp between QCL and Z, but were simply presented with these two choices, we would opt for the readings 'fácil' and 'campean' on the principle of 'lectio difficilior melius'. That is, we would choose the more difficult word on the assumption that an unauthorised change is much more likely to go in the direction difficult-to-easy than vice-versa. The authenticity of the readings would of course need to be supported, as in these two cases, by Calderón's use of the words elsewhere.

So far, so good; but, as already indicated, these principles do not absolve us from the need to think and, indeed, do not always solve the problems for us. For example, in one of the well-known speeches at the beginning of the play, Rosaura refers to Segismundo's tower thus:

> Rustico nace entre desnudas peñas
> un Palacio tan breve,
> que el Sol apenas à mirar se atreve.   (QCL, 56-8)

Later, Clarín puts forward the suggestion that

> es mejor que la gente
> que habita en ella, generosamente
> nos admita.   (QCL, 67-9)

There is no feminine noun to which 'ella' can refer. If we look at Z, we can see what happened:

> Rustica yaze entre eleuadas peñas
> vna torre tan breue,
> que lince el Sol a verla no se atreue.[62]

The application of Greg's principles will lead us to conclude that Calderón himself revised lines 56-8; there is a nice irony (which will become apparent later) in the use of 'Palacio', and even 'nace' is

---

62. References to *La vida es sueño* are to Sloman's edition (see note 60); *La cisma de Ingalaterra* is quoted from the edition of F. Ruiz Ramón (Madrid, 1981).

more in keeping with the preoccupations of the play. However, if Calderón revised line 68 to take account of the change in gender of the key noun, his revision has not reached us; in fact it is more likely that he overlooked it. If we change 'ella' to 'él', we need a hiatus to produce eleven syllables; what are we to do? The answer must be that we retain 'ella', since we have no evidence that Calderón ever wrote 'él', and that we draw attention to the problem in a note. This is a 'solution' which the editor will often find himself obliged to adopt.

Sometimes the editor will find problems more intractable than this. Sometimes he will find that no versions exist which can be used to correct flaws in the basic text (there may be only one surviving version, or all the versions may be obviously wrong). In such cases the editor should consider making the correction on his own authority. At the simplest level, this may involve putting right an obvious misprint, but other, more complex corrections are bound to arise. The editor will be less likely to err if he bears four points in mind: 1) modification of the readings of a basic text should not be undertaken lightly; 2) no editor should adopt a reading from a version other than the basic text without some idea of how the reading reached that version and without some evidence that it could be authentic; 3) where there are two readings of apparently equal authority, it is better to adopt the one which can be supported from other occurrences in the author's work; and 4) if the editor concludes that the correct reading is not present in any surviving version in which the author might have intervened, but that he or another editor has reconstructed it, he should at least consider what mechanism produced the error from what he thinks is the correct reading (i.e. misprint, misreading or any of the other causes mentioned earlier); if the error is inexplicable, he should think again.[63]

63. For example, C.A. Jones suggested in his edition of *El médico de su honra* (Oxford, 1961) that the reading 'viendo' in line 1369 ought to be 'huyendo' and that the error arose because Calderón's spelling was 'vyendo'. This seemed only a guess, but the explanation is supported by the fact that Calderón used this spelling for 'huyendo' in the autograph manuscript of *Polifemo y Circe*.

5 *Deciding what kind of edition to produce*

Editors of classical English plays have access to a number of series in which their editions may be published. These series usually have general editors who exercise a close control over the kind of edition which is produced. For practical purposes this situation does not operate in the field of Spanish drama. As a consequence, decisions about the kind of edition to be produced are largely to be taken by the individual editor.[64]

The editor's options are theoretically numerous, but can be reduced to three basic ones : 1) an edition which preserves all the accidentals of the basic text (spelling, capitalisation, accentuation, punctuation, lineation); 2) an edition which preserves some accidentals but not all of them; 3) an edition which modernises all the accidentals. Until the twentieth century, an editor would hardly even consider producing a text with the original accidentals. As the century has advanced, more and more editions have been produced with some of the accidentals (usually spelling) preserved; there are still relatively few which retain all the accidentals.[65] Since we are dealing here with printed sources, it is as well to reiterate the crucial point that in a printed edition the author's original accidentals will already have been modified.

An author's original accidentals are sacrosanct only in so far as they are a guide to what the author intended to say, and as a source of information for editors of other plays. If his accidentals are eccentric both by his contemporary and our own modern standards, no editor can be expected to retain all of them once he has extracted his information from them and made a note of them for the enlightenment of other editors. For example, in lines 13-14 of Act III of his play *En la vida todo es verdad y todo mentira,* Calderón wrote:

hasta que .de. otra ylusion
de sus pasiones yndicio

64. Of course series such as Castalia expect editors to follow certain norms in the introduction and typographical style; but they are free, for example, to use modern or old-style accidentals for texts of plays.
65. Only the Hamburg Calderoniana series, under the direction of Prof. Flasche, has tried to retain all accidentals when working from printed copy-texts.

The points before and after the first 'de' were evidently meant to indicate a verb in the subjunctive as opposed to a preposition; an efficient seventeenth-century compositor would have omitted them in favour of an accent on the 'e', just as a modern editor should. But how to decide between the accidentals of an efficient seventeenth-century compositor and modern practice, when these vary? Here we must weigh up the losses and gains.

The accidentals of printed Spanish in the Golden Age were essentially rhetorical rather than the product of grammatical logic, as is now the case. That is, they were more concerned to preserve the emphases of speech than to aid the thought-processes of the modern silent reader, as this quotation suggests:

> es de saber que enel razonamiẽto, y comun hablar nuestro, acostumbramos hazer (como cada vno vee) ciertas pausas, o detenciones: y estos [*sic*] siruen assi para que descãse el que habla, como para que entienda el que escucha. Y es de notar que no se haze pausa dõde quiera, o siempre que al que habla se le antoja, antes bien en cierto lugar y paradero, que es en fin de sentencia perfecta, o imperfecta: y desta perfection o imperfection nasce ser mayor o menor la pausa y descanso del que habla. Como la escriptura no sea otra cosa que vn razonamiento y platica con los ausentes, hallan se tãbiẽ enella las mismas pausas y interuallos señalados con diuersas maneras de rayas, y pũtos.[66]

A system of accidentals intended to preserve the emphases of speech cannot but be relevant to the editor of a *play*. An editor should therefore devote serious thought to preserving the two accidentals involved, i.e. punctuation and capitalisation. If his projected edition is of the scholarly kind, then preservation is extremely desirable; but if it is 'popular', then preservation of these

---

66. Yciar, *Arte subtilissima*, L3[r] + [v]. It is instructive to compare the accidentals (especially punctuation) of this revised version with that of 1548. In this case we have reason to suppose that Yciar himself made the revisions. The 'estos' error results from the fact that in the first version the masculine 'interuallos' was used instead of 'detenciones'. This careless, incomplete revision is the same as Calderón's failure to change 'en ella' to correspond with 'Palacio'. Both errors help to show which version is the earlier (although Yciar's error might be confused with a misprint if we did not already know which version was the earlier).

accidentals may be regarded as eccentric and even counterproductive.

Spelling is in a somewhat different category, in that the original compositors tended to preserve far more of the author's own than of the other accidentals. Complete modernisation of spelling is always undesirable, for it will obscure distinctions or similarities of rhyme and metre which should be preserved. Thus if we add 'p' or 'c' to 'conceto' or 'perfeto', they will no longer rhyme with 'discreto'; if we modernise 'mesmo' to 'mismo', it will no longer assonate with 'lecho'; if we change Calderón's spellings 'agora' and 'aora' to modern 'ahora', we disguise the fact that he always used the first for three syllables, the second for two; if we change 'Ingalaterra' or 'corónica' to the versions now current, we may create short lines, and so on. Even in cases where rhyme and metre are not involved, we may spoil jokes and puns, as in the case of Sancho's remark about 'el yelmo de malino', where modernisation to 'maligno' obscures the already feeble joke.[67] Even in popular editions, therefore, some spellings must be retained. The editor can adopt one of two rules: 1) retain all spellings where modernisation might adversely affect either the meaning or the metre, or 2) retain all spellings which might imply a pronunciation different from that implied by modern spelling. The second of these is probably preferable, since it is safer: even a careful editor may fail to notice puns or jokes. However, even the second rule is potentially imperfect, for there will be cases where differing spellings have the same pronunciation, and modernisation can help to obscure a point. In a scholarly edition this problem can be largely avoided by preserving the original spelling.[68]

In all cases involving spelling, punctuation and capitalisation, the editor who intends to retain the originals must be prepared to correct them. He may even find it necessary to choose a different copy-text for accidentals as opposed to substantives.

---

67. Cf. Flores, *The Compositors...Part I*, p. 45n and p. 47.

68. For example, the words 'hay' and '¡ay!' were usually both written 'ay'; the scanty punctuation of the seventeenth century does not always distinguish them. Even if he retains 'ay', however, the old-spelling editor will need to remind his reader in cases where ambiguity is possible.

That is, there may be one version which is unquestionably the best from the point of view of substantives, but which has inadequate punctuation, or which changes the perfectly acceptable spelling of the author in ways which adversely affect metre, rhyme or deliberate ambiguity, as already described. Another version, demonstrably inferior in its substantives, may preserve desirable spellings and have accurate punctuation. In such cases it will not merely be sensible but also correct procedure to adopt one version for substantives and the other for accidentals. An editor will find it relatively easy to familiarise himself with the 'rules' of Golden-Age spelling, punctuation and capitalisation, and thus to make proper corrections when necessary. He will only be doing what the original compositors ought to have done in the first place.

Accentuation and lineation fall into a different category from the other accidentals. In the case of lineation, two practices were current in the Golden Age. In one, each line of verse was given one line on the page, and lines which were shared between several speakers had the speakers' names added in the usual italics between the spoken words. The other method was to give every new speaker a new line, beginning always in the left-hand margin. Our modern method is more similar to the second, except that we indent the speeches of second or subsequent speakers in any one line by an amount corresponding to the words already spoken. There is nothing to be gained by adopting either of the two old systems here, especially since choice between them was often governed by the space available. Editors may also, if they wish, indent the opening line of each stanza of a particular form of verse. This was not normally done in verse plays in the Golden Age, but there are precedents for it in printed verse of the period. There is one case where editors should exercise special care: certain verse-forms, e.g. dodecasyllables, could be set down in long lines (regular dodecasyllables) or as pairs of short ones (two hexasyllables). (This is especially true of some of Calderón's later plays.) Again, compositorial practice was often influenced by the availability of space, so editors must try to discover (from manuscripts) the habits of their author. Failure to do so will affect the identification of verse-forms and the numbering of lines, which in turn may produce differences in metrical statistics.

As for accents, we have seen how an author might omit them, preferring instead quite eccentric methods of indicating that they should be present. Compositors were expected to put them in, although they did not always do so, even when the proper type was available. Editors clearly ought to put them in. As for choosing between Golden-Age and modern systems of accentuation, there is no cogent reason for not adopting the clearer modern system, for possible ambiguities will have to be eliminated under both. That is, a good compositor was expected to distinguish between 'amàra' (subjunctive) and 'amarà' (future) by using accents as shown; or to distinguish between 'hàcia' (preposition) and 'hacia' (verb, which was not given an accent). Bad compositors might not bother, and misguided ones might put accents in the wrong place. The modern system will force some additional choices on the editor, such as that between 'continua' (adjective) and 'continúa' (verb), which were not normally differentiated under the old system. The point is that both systems may call on the editor to make a choice between alternatives. He will need to identify the cases where two readings are genuinely possible, and choose between them on the basis of what he knows of the author's style. Where real doubt still remains, he must have recourse to a note.

As already indicated, the nature of the copy-text and other useful texts will help the editor to decide what kind of edition he is going to produce. If a text shows signs of having been set from the author's manuscript by one faithful compositor, so that much of the original spelling and capitalisation has been consistently preserved, this will be a good reason for retaining these accidentals. If, on the other hand, the editor's copy-text is far removed from the original and has been set by two or more compositors of widely differing habits and competence, there is little point in preserving the inconsistency of the accidentals. The wisest procedure is to point out the inconsistencies, deduce what can be deduced from them, and modernise. The same will hold good for cases where the editor has to make use of different versions of his text to provide corrections. There are texts where a whole act needs to be taken from a different version (Calderón's *Los cabellos de Absalón* is one such). In the latter case it would be legitimate to preserve the variant accidentals (Calderón's for two of the acts, Tirso's for the other), or for any play written by more than one author; but when great variation is not authorial, the wisest plan will be to standardise by modernising—as, for example, J.M. Ruano has recently done in *Cada uno para sí*.[69] However, if only a few lines or words have to be taken from another version, there is no good reason why the editor should not modify their accidentals to match whatever system he has decided to adopt, old or new. One would do it without a second thought when producing a modernised text, so why not do so in a text with the old accidentals?

6 *Deciding how much and what kind of editorial apparatus to include*

This question depends to a large extent on the kind of audience the editor has in mind for his edition. As part of his introduction, every editor, even of a popular edition, should state what his basis was. He should also provide a textual bibliography, even if it is only a list of the important editions. An editor who hopes to produce a definitive edition must reveal the evidence behind these simple statements. He needs to show why he has picked his copy-text, and why he has adopted readings from this or that other version. That is, he must prove relationships between texts. If these texts are particularly scarce, or have never been properly described, he will need to describe them, and to indicate which copy or copies he has examined. If no adequate bibliography already exists, it is up to him to provide one, as fully as possible. Other matters of a partly bibliographical nature which should be dealt with are the date of the play and the statistical information deriving from the play.

Statistical information has traditionally involved only versification. More and more research is being done on verse-forms, and an editor can save investigators a great deal of time if he provides a metrical analysis based on his definitive edition. However, there are other useful statistics besides this: the number of characters, male and female, and the proportions of words spoken by them, and in what metres; or, more ambitiously,

69. See p. 140 of his edition of Kassel, 1982.

statistics produced with the aid of a computer. The simplest, and most economical in terms of space, is a word frequency count, a list which simply says that 'a' occurs 500 times, 'abuela' twice, and so on. This is not much use unless it includes references, so that the reader can examine the context. Even this minor addition can add greatly to the space required, for common words will have many entries. A word frequency count with references is called a word list. The next stage is a concordance, i.e. a word list which gives contexts. In a volume which already includes the text, this is a luxury, for it will take up as much space again. Of more use will be a reverse index, which lists the words in reverse order of their letters. This will aid those who want to investigate rhymes, or who want to undertake linguistic analyses, e.g. involving the use of tenses which can be identified by word endings, the use of plural nouns, adverbs ending in -mente, and the like.

Some of the statistics mentioned above may throw light on the date of the play. If the date is already known, it will make these statistics more useful. Sometimes the date of the first edition will be a guide to the date of the play. Other matters which may throw light on the date are the life of the author, current events, the sources of the play, the manner of its staging, its subject-matter, the names of its characters, its style and vocabulary. All of these things should be investigated in an edition which pretends to be definitive. Traditionally, the editor is also expected to provide an interpretation of the play. However, since literary criticism is not definitive, the editor of a definitive edition need not feel bound by this tradition, particularly if he has to omit something in the definitive category to accommodate it. If a critical interpretation is included, its usefulness will be much enhanced if it refers to and evaluates any earlier criticism which may exist.

The editor must also decide how much textual apparatus to present. The apparatus will include records of variants, and explanatory notes. If possible, substantive and accidental variants should be kept separate. The editor should have a clear idea (preferably a definition) of what constitutes a substantive variant before he begins to collate his texts. One definition is 'a reading which alters the sound or sense of a word, or which alters the number of words in the text'. This will distinguish between 'escuro' and 'oscuro', 'deso' and 'de eso', which may not be necessary in all kinds of editions; editors can introduce exceptions or modifications to suit their own needs. There is no point in listing variants from editions which have no authority, unless they can provide information for other editors. (For example, editors comparing an original Calderón *parte* with the Vera Tassis version will see that Vera often introduced elegant but unauthoritative changes such as 'juzgar' and 'encontrar' for 'pensar' and 'topar'. It may seem useless to record these, since they are simply wrong, but the information may help editors of texts for which Vera is the only or principal source.) As for accidentals, lists of variants tend to be long, and to be consulted by very few. A lot of space can be saved if the editor records only his departures from the accidentals of the copy-text, and those which alter the sense; there is little to be gained by recording variant but 'equally correct' accidentals. In a modernised text, the only variant accidentals which matter are those which alter the sense.

Explanatory notes will deal with obscure passages, allusions, archaisms and the like. In this respect they will often serve to justify the editor in his choice of readings. However, if the editor feels the need to provide frequent explanation or justification for his choices, he should consider providing a separate series of textual notes. All these notes—variant notes, explanatory notes, textual notes—can appear as footnotes, but as printing costs increase, it is becoming more usual to print them in appendix form, particularly the last two. This is not to say that the editor should eschew the true appendix, which can be used for transcriptions of long variant passages, of rare or special source-texts, or of documents which have some bearing on the play. These are best transcribed verbatim, unedited. If they contain errors, these can be followed by [*sic*] and perhaps by a suggested correction, followed by a query.

Finally, if he wishes, the editor can supply an index to his notes (or to annotated words), a list of works cited, and a list of suitable further reading. The first is most useful to scholars, the second almost essential, the third most useful to students. If there is any room for illustrations, prints from the copy-text or of pertinent rare documents are always valuable.

7 *Doing the actual editing*

One of the best ways to begin the job of editing a text is to take a copy (xerox if necessary) of the best modern edition and read it through, marking textual problems, difficult passages, passages which will need notes, and so on. The modern ranges of fluorescent highlighter pens, with their wide choice of colours, are ideal for this. Eventually all potentially important versions of the text must be examined, preferably in some sort of xerographic form, with wide margins for notes. Variants may be noted in these margins, if there are not too many, or on separate sheets or on cards. Cards are best, since they make the insertion of omissions easy. They are also ideal, in their larger sizes, for recording explanatory notes and works to be consulted. By the time the editor has examined and compared the other versions of his text, the number of highlighted words and phrases will have increased greatly.

As a working draft, the editor will find it convenient to use a marked-up xerox print of his copy-text. An editor who is preparing a modernised edition can continue to use the copy of his modern edition (if one exists). Sooner or later, however, it is best to type out the play, in order to avoid being excessively influenced by the basic text. Before typing begins, the editor should have decided how to indicate that he is incorporating variants into his text, and how to record the significant variants he is not going to incorporate. He will also have decided how he is going to present speakers' names and stage directions, and how he is going to deal with the abbreviations which occur in these and in his text proper.

There are two basic schools of thought. One argues that the text should be left uncluttered. The other accepts that a definitive edition is already specialised, and makes free use of brackets in the text, with a saving in notes. Thus the second school announces in a preface that all abbreviations (*Fed.* as a speaker's name, q̃, amãdo, etc.) have been resolved with the help of square brackets, and no further note is necessary (so we find *Fed* [*erico*], q[ue], ama[n]do, etc., and know what has happened). Adopted variants also get square brackets, although these need a note to say where the reading came from and what the original was. Letters or words which are unnecessarily present are enclosed in round brackets;

thus 'ama(n)do' rhymes with 'dado', and does not need a note to say so. We have seen that the use of abbreviations can help to identify compositors. If this is relevant to his own text, the editor will already have studied the matter; if it may be relevant to other editors (e.g. of other plays in the same volume), he should remember that his colleagues may find it just as easy to go back to the original as to consult his edition. If the unique copy of the original is in Timbuktu Public Library, he can still note abbreviations in an appendix, in tabulated form. As for the adoption of variant readings, if these are recorded in a footnote, there is no absolute need to mark their presence in the text by using square brackets. In other words, ways can be found of avoiding the addition of extraneous brackets to the text. Editors must make up their own minds about this, but if they hope that their play will be read with enthusiasm by others besides fellow editors, they should give serious thought to keeping their texts as uncluttered as possible.

The seventeenth-century way of presenting speakers' names and stage directions is still one of the best. That is, italics are used for both. Speakers' names go in the left-hand margin, long stage directions between the lines of text, centred, and short stage directions in the right-hand margin. There are other ways, most of them quite acceptable. As for the recording of variants, there are again various styles, but the best ones are those which use least punctuation. One of the simplest ways is to give a line-reference to the text as edited, followed by a quotation of the word or words in that text which are subject to variation (the 'lemma'). This quotation is closed by a square bracket and followed by the quotation of the variant, as it appears in the original. Finally an abbreviation (or abbreviations) is added (the 'siglum', plural 'sigla') to indicate which text or texts contain the variant. Example: 1234 siendo] si ando VT. This indicates that in line 1234 the reading of the copy-text, 'siendo', has been retained, but that the Vera Tassis edition reads 'si ando'. If we had 1234 siendo] si ando P-VT, it would mean that the *parte* text had the 'si ando' reading, and that 'siendo' had been adopted from Vera Tassis.[70]

70. For a detailed explanation, see Ruano's edition of *Cada uno para sí*, pp. 140-1.

As much as possible of the 'obvious' editing should have been done before the typing starts. That is, the editor will already have decided (on the basis of information deriving from the stemma) which variants he is certainly going to adopt, and which he is certainly going to reject, and he will have marked up his draft accordingly. There will be other variants about which he is uncertain. At this stage he need only make provisional decisions about them and about those cases where the inadequacy of all existing texts may force him to offer a 'variant' of his own. Whenever the basic text is changed by the adoption of a variant, the change should be noted for incorporation in the notes.

When the 'obvious' editorial changes have been marked in the working draft, the typescript can be produced. When it is complete, it should be checked thoroughly, preferably by at least two people. Then, without the presence of his copy-text, but with the aid of his variant lists, the editor should go through the typescript again, making a final assessment of the 'uncertain' variants, considering the places where his text may be improved, and examining his variant lists to see if there are any possibly authoritative readings which might serve the purpose; and he should ask himself if all his accidentals are sensible and consistent. This process will act as a further check on the typing. If it can also be done by a colleague who has a good knowledge of Golden-Age drama but no preconceptions about the text in question, so much the better.

When this examination is finished, the typescript may well be covered in alterations, and the editor may feel obliged to retype it before presenting it to his publishers. It should be remembered that every fresh typing *inevitably* introduces fresh errors, and that modern compositors are better than we suppose at working from heavily marked-up copy. The answer, if there is one available, is to use a word-processor. This makes it possible to insert alterations and corrections as they arise, without the introduction of fresh errors. The poor editor's alternative is one of the proprietary brands of typewriter correcting fluid.

Once the text has been typed and checked, and line-numbers added, the rest of the edition follows. Since both the introduction and the notes refer to and sometimes quote from the text, it is pointless to try to produce a final version of them until the text is completed. The bibliography can be left until last, but as he is typing the introduction and notes, the editor will find it useful to note on his file cards, with the appropriate page number of his typescript, every occasion when a work is referred to. This will make it simpler to give a full reference on the first occasion, and a consistently abbreviated reference on subsequent occasions. The marked cards will then constitute the list of works referred to, and will provide the basis for any list of abbreviations used. Quotations from and references to the most readily available works can be checked for the last time in typescript.

*   *   *   *   *

Editors are sure to encounter difficulties which have been inadequately dealt with above. When they do, they will do well to remember that the science of editing classical plays is considerably more advanced in the field of English than of Spanish literature. Almost all the problems they encounter will already have been met and sometimes tackled by counterparts in English. This being so, the best advice that can be given, should a specific problem arise, is to consult the excellent index of *The Library* (The Transactions of the Bibliographical Society). The circumstances governing the writing, performance and publication of Spanish Golden-Age drama, while unique, have more in common with those of contemporary England than with those of any other European country. It would be a foolish Hispanist who did not take advantage of this fact.[71]

71. For purposes of comparison, readers may care to look at Clifford Leech, 'On Editing One's First Play', SB, 23 (1970), 61-70. Those who wish to pursue comparisons further should read Fredson Bowers, 'Today's Shakespeare Texts, and Tomorrow's', SB, 19 (1966), 39-65. Being twenty years old (delivered in 1964), this lecture is no longer a complete reflection of the state of Shakespearean textual scholarship; but editors of Spanish Golden-Age drama will find that in many areas their discipline still lags behind the Shakespearean scholarships of 1964. For some recent views on old spelling, see *Play-texts in Old Spelling: Papers from the Glendon Conference*, ed. R.C. Shady and G.B. Shand (London, 1983).

THE USES OF POLYMETRY: AN APPROACH TO EDITING THE *COMEDIA* AS VERSE DRAMA

Victor Dixon

Any text we may edit was originally a message to an expected reader; but a dramatic text, a script, is best regarded—like a recipe, a blueprint or a musical score—as a set of instructions to a number of executants, by means of whose interpretative collaboration it is to be 'realised' and presented to its public. Even if in Golden-Age Spain literary texts of every other kind were probably still intended for performance, aloud, to an audience,[1] production in a theatre, by a company of actors who visibly, physically bodied forth the characters, must have been intrinsically different. Of course at many times and places, including sixteenth-century Spain, texts have been written in dramatic form which

---

[1] See for instance Margit Frenk, 'Lectores y oidores. La difusión oral de la literatura en el siglo de oro', in *Actas del VII Congreso de la Asociación Internacional de Hispanistas* (Rome, 1982), I, 101-23.

were not destined to be performed;[2] and many of the seventeenth-century *comedias* which have survived were printed to be read rather than acted. Juan Pérez de Montalbán, for instance, asserted that he published his plays not only to provide the public with accurate, properly attributed texts, but so that they could be coolly and carefully assessed by readers: 'para que las censureis en vuestro aposento, que aunque parecieron razonablemente en el tablado, no es credito seguro; porque tal vez el ademan de la dama, la representacion del Heroè, la cadencia de las vozes, el ruydo de las consonantes, y la suspension de los afectos, suelen engañar las orejas mas atentas, y hazer que passen por rayos los relampagos.'[3] This had patently not been, however, his original intention, and *comedias* had invariably been performed before they were published. As Lope wrote of those in his *Novena parte*: 'Es verdad que no las escribí con este ánimo, ni para que de los oídos del teatro se trasladaran a la censura de los aposentos.'[4] In any case, of course, a seventeenth-century reader would himself have 'realised' the *comedia*, as the author had written it, in terms of *corral* conditions, in his mind's eye and ear. So, we must hope, will our twentieth-century students; and it is our job as editors not only to provide, so far as possible, a clear and accurate text of the 'ideal version...that which the author sent to the theatre for performance',[5] but to assist them, by the way in which we present it, in its imaginative recreation.

This is a matter, as well as of its visualisation, of (to coin a phrase) its 'auralisation'. Some recent critics, indeed, have heavily emphasised the auditory nature of the *comedia*. They have reminded us that the dramatist was most frequently called a *poeta*, the actors *recitantes* and the spectators *oyentes*. For John G. Weiger, 'la comedia española es una forma de arte para el oído, o sea, un género auditivo... Para Lope, la comedia consiste ante todo

[2] See Ronald E. Surtz, *The Birth of a Theater: Dramatic Convention in the Spanish Theater from Juan del Encina to Lope de Vega* (Princeton, 1979), Chapter VI, pp. 149-74.

[3] Juan Pérez de Montalbán, *Primero tomo de las comedias* (Alcalá, 1638), fol.11 verso.

[4] Quoted by Frenk, p. 122, note 86.

[5] Edward M. Wilson, 'The two editions of Calderón's *Primera parte* of 1640', *The Library*, V, xiv (1959), 175-91 (p. 191).

en los elementos que escuchará el público.'[6] Margit Frenk has described it as the 'género oído y comunitario por excelencia', has said that 'por lo menos hasta 1630-40, la parte espectacular del teatro, todo lo que percibía la vista, casi no contaba: el público iba a los corrales para oír.... Sólo con [Calderón] y con la inauguración del teatro del Buen Retiro comienza a cobrar más importancia el aspecto visual de las comedias.'[7] Alicia Amadei-Pulice has gone even further: 'La intelección de una obra como *Fuenteovejuna* o *Los embustes de Fabia* no pierde nada si se escucha a ojos cerrados. En la 'especie' *comedia* de Lope la dimensión visual está ausente'.[8] This is frankly absurd. The advent of *apariencias*, of *máquinas*, or *carpintería*, of Italianate spectacle, undoubtedly influenced the interrelationship between the aural and the visual; but a proper appreciation of their impact demands an awareness of the semiology of the *corral*, of the brilliance with which the best plays written for it (including most of Calderón's most famous) exploited, as well as its structure, its limited but often eloquent visual resources: costume, properties, movement, gesture...They spoke to ear and eye at once in complementary languages, combining for instance (to echo Maurice Charney) both verbal and 'presentational' imagery.[9] The *comedia*, in Luis de Morales Polo's phrase, is 'un convite que el entendimiento hace al oído y a la vista';[10] and Juan de Zabaleta, writing as late as 1660 but about a visit to the *corral*, imagines as follows what may happen to two female spectators: 'La que está junto a la puerta de la caçuela, oye a los representantes, y no los ve. La que está en el banco último los ve y no los oye, con que ninguna ve la comedia; porque las comedias ni se oyen sin ojos ni se ven sin oídos; las acciones hablan gran

---

[6] John G. Weiger, *Hacia la comedia: de los valencianos a Lope* (Madrid, 1978), pp.43, 46.

[7] Frenk, p. 113 and note.

[8] Alicia Amadei-Pulice, '*El stile rapprasentativo* en la *comedia de teatro* de Calderón', in *Approaches to the Theater of Calderón*, edited by Michael D. McGaha (Washington, 1982), pp. 215-29 (pp. 218-9).

[9] Maurice Charney, *Shakespeare's Roman Plays: The Function of Imagery in the Drama* (Harvard, 1961). On the semiology of the *corral*, see especially José María Díez Borque, *Sociedad y teatro en la España de Lope de Vega* (Barcelona, 1978), pp. 208-46.

[10] Luis de Morales Polo, *Epítome de los hechos y dichos del Emperador Trajano* (1654), quoted in M. Menéndez y Pelayo, *Historia de las ideas estéticas en España* (Buenos Aires, 1943), I, 316 note.

parte, y sino se oyen las palabras, son las acciones mudas.'[11]

I might argue at length that modern critics should adopt a similarly balanced approach, as indeed did Lope de Vega;[12] but my brief at the moment is in fact to concede and stress the aural impact of the *comedia*—or rather one aspect of that impact. Too little, sad to say, has been written of the use of sound effects and offstage noises in Golden-Age plays,[13] or indeed of the function of music and song;[14] rather more has been said, by critics like Edward Wilson, Bruce Wardropper and David Gitlitz, of the poetic content of the spoken word, of the exploitation of imagery and techniques derived from poetic tradition.[15] But my present concern is with the manipulation of poetic form, of the expressive metrical diversity which is characteristic of Golden-Age plays. It can hardly be overstressed that the *comedia* speaks not only in verse but in a rich variety of verse forms. Indeed, if metrical flexibility is to be accounted a virtue, it is one in which no national drama before or since can compete with that of Spain.

Not all critics, of course, have so regarded it; in fact the most dedicated student of *comedia* versification, S.G. Morley, was surpirisngly unenthusiastic. Recognizing that 'the language of drama is never exactly that of real life', and 'there are all stages of convention in dramatic dialogue', and commenting on the eleven metres employed in *El castigo sin venganza* that 'no other drama known to me can exhibit anything like this variety', he nevertheless

---

[11] Juan de Zabaleta, *El día de fiesta por la tarde* (1660), edited by J.M. Díez Borque (Madrid, 1977), p. 34.

[12] We can discern as much, for instance, from a *careful* reading of the *Prólogo dialogístico* in his *Decimasexta parte* (Madrid, 1621); see also F.A. de Armas, 'Italian Canvases in Lope de Vega's *comedias*: the case of *Venus and Adonis'*, *CH*, 2 (1980), 135-42.

[13] See Henri Recoules, 'Ruidos y efectos sonores en el teatro del siglo de oro', *BRAE*, 55 (1975), 109-45.

[14] See however, especially, Gustavo Umpierre, *Songs in the Plays of Lope de Vega* (London, 1975), and Jack Sage, '*The Function of Music in the Theatre of Calderón*' in *The comedias of Calderón*, edited by D.W. Cruickshank and J.E. Varey (London, 1973), XIX, 209-30.

[15] See especially Edward M. Wilson, 'Images et structure dans *Peribáñez'*, *BH*, 51 (1949), 125-59; Bruce W. Wardropper, 'The Implicit Craft of the Spanish *Comedia'*, in *Studies in Spanish Literature of the Golden Age presented to Edward M. Wilson*, edited by R.O. Jones (London, 1973), pp. 339-56: David M. Gitlitz, *La estructura lírica de la comedia de Lope de Vega* (Valencia, 1980).

patently preferred either prose or prosy poetry—English blank verse, or the French alexandrine—to 'the more elaborate and artificial patters of the lyric', on the ground that use of the latter constituted 'an evident breach of reality in ostensible imitation of reality'.[16] His views may win the agreement of those who believe that the *comedia* aspired to realism—or that it should have done so; but others will feel here an insensitivity to changing concepts of verisimilitude and changing attitudes to 'psychical distance'.[17]

The neo-classical López Pinciano seems to have been more open-minded than Morley. His interlocutors declare repeatedly, it is true, that verse itself is always unnaturalistic, so that prose is more than acceptable in comedy; it is a matter of *verosimilitud* versus *deleite*. Yet they also declare, repeatedly, that 'cada vno puede hazer lo que quisiere en este particular sin cometer yerro alguno', that both tragedy and comedy may use all kinds of metres, and interestingly advocate the use of different verse forms for different purposes: 'Y de la comedia misma digo que recibe toda suerte de metros qual la tragedia, mas no conuiene contenga muchos de los endecasylabos, ni tampoco canciones; porque, como las personas son baxas, no está bien que usen de metros altos muchos; y en lo de las canciones digo no conuienen, porque son rimas muy fuera del común vso de hablar, y la comedia dévese aplicar mucho al vso común. De aquí nace que los antiguos vsaron mucho los jambos, y a nosotros nos estarán bien las redondillas'.[18] Closer to Morley's view was that of the eighteenth-century neo-classicist Luzán; he found Lope's metrics inconsistent with 'la verosimilitud que el mismo Lope encarga al poeta; porque ciertamente no parece verosímil que las personas de la comedia se expliquen en versos tan artificiosos; ni con ellos se imita bien la plática, esto es, la conversación familiar de dos o tres personas'.[19]

---

[16] Sylvanus G. Morley, 'The Curious Phenomenon of Spanish Verse Drama', *BH*, 50 (1948), 445-62.

[17] See Edward Bullogh, 'Psychical Distance as a Factor in Art and an Aesthetic Principle', *British Journal of Psychology* 5 (1912), 87-118; and compare Suzanne K. Langer, *Feeling and Form* (London, 1953), Chapter 17, The Dramatic Illusion.

[18] Alonso López Pinciano, *Philosophia antigua poetica* (1596), edited by Alfredo Carballo Picazo (Madrid, 1973), I, 205-07; II, 221-22, 286-88.

[19] Ignacio de Luzán, *La poética*, edited by Isabel M. Cid de Sirgado (Madrid, 1974), p. 321 (Book III, Chapter 2, edition of 1789).

Lúzan was critical, similarly, of the plays of Juan de la Cueva: 'Todas están escritas con estancias líricas, siguen con octavas, después redondillas y tercetos, alternando estas versificaciones, y nunca romance; porque Cueva no conoció el que tan acertadamente usaron los escritores cómicos más modernos.'[20] In fact Spanish dramatists of the eighteenth century (following a tendency already apparent in the seventeenth) found *romances*, or the hendecasyllabic *romances históricos*, with their merely assonantal rhyme in every other line, the most acceptable alternative to realistic prose. The Romantics revived the lyric forms of the Golden Age, but experiments like Bretón de los Herreros' *Marcela* were rare. Rarer still were defences of polymetry like that of Juan Nicolás Böhl de Faber: 'Si no se puede negar que el metro tiene alguna relación con el sentido de las palabras, y si no es menos cierto que en el teatro no sólo se expresan los afectos, sino que se relatan los sucedidos, se hacen descripciones y se versan argumentos, ¿quién pudo condenar el uso de varios metros correspondientes a tan distintos objetos, sino un ciego idólatra de la pobreza y monotonía de la versificación francesa?'[21]

Alfred Morel-Fatio, in his commentary on the *Arte nuevo*, rebutted Luzán's objections to Lope's versification, declaring similarly that the alexandrine was monotonous and no more verisimilar than Spanish *redondillas*; but here and elsewhere he himself criticized 'l'emploi d'une versification plus lyrique que dramatique et qu'on ne doit pas hésiter de qualifier de puérile ... Qu'un monologue s'enferme dans les quatorze vers d'un sonnet, qu'un dialogue s'échange en cascades de rédondilles...voilà bien de quoi causer, surtout dans les pièces de caractère tragique, une impression directement opposée à celle que l'auteur entendait produire...passé les monts, cette versification d'opéra n'est pas facilement admise et porte à la comedia une préjudice considérable.'[22] The reference to opera was clearly meant to be pejorative (though for some of us *Le nozze di Figaro* is the supreme

---

[20] Luzán, p. 297 (Book III, Chapter I, edition of 1789).

[21] Quoted by Alfred Morel-Fatio, 'L'*Arte nuevo de hazer comedias en este tiempo* de Lope de Vega', *BH*, 3 (1901), 364-405 (p. 401).

[22] Morel-Fatio, *op. cit.*, p. 398, and *La comedia espagnole au 17e siècle* (Paris, 1923), p. 64.

achievement of *homo sapiens*), but there are illuminating analogies, as Montesinos pointed out, between that most stylized and artificial of dramatic forms and the *comedia de corral*—let alone, of course, the palace entertainments which were to evolve alongside it: 'Es increíble la cantidad de ocasiones en que la comedia española nos hace pensar en la ópera, que de algún modo fue su heredera.'[23] The drama of Golden-Age Spain is a *dramma lirico*.

It is not surprising, therefore, to learn that Richard Wagner admired the polymetry of the *comedia* (although its metres were presumably much modified in the translations he read); he criticized, it appears, a work by Goethe: 'Le falta la conclusión, porque todas las estrofas son iguales y no encuentra la alternancia entre los versos de dos y tres pies: esto se ha perdido, lo que los griegos sabían tan bien y que me sorprendió en mi juventud, permitiéndome construir toda mi métrica. Lope de Vega conocía esta alternancia, pero Calderón no tan bien: él razonaba demasiado y utilizaba en su lugar un troqueo uniforme.'[24]

Wagner's reference to the Greeks recalls another analogy, reminds us that Spanish polymetry 'is foreshadowed by the Greek tragedians' use of different types of metre for the choral and dramatic elements of their plays'.[25] Indeed we may go further, and say that Greek tragedy, without directly influencing the *comedia*, probably anticipated it in the exploitation of metrical variety as an expressive resource. The different modes of the music which accompanied song and dance in their theatre were agreed by the Greeks to have different emotional and ethical effects on their hearers, and to be more or less suitable to the nature and mood of certain passages. But in the greatest period of the Athenian drama it was the words which were supreme, and these were part of a

---

[23] J. Fernández Montesinos, 'La paradoja del *Arte nuevo*', in *Estudios sobre Lope de Vega* (Salamanca, 1969), pp. 1-20 (p. 15).

[24] Quoted by Jordi Mota, 'Wagner y el teatro clásico español', *Nueva Estafeta*, Nos. 45-46 (August-September 1982), 54-61 (p. 59). I have failed so far to identify the letter in which these remarks were made.

[25] Duncan Moir, 'The Classical Tradition in Spanish Dramatic Theory and Practice', in *Classical Drama and its Influence, Essays presented to H.D.F. Kitto*, edited by M.J. Anderson (London, 1965), pp. 191-228 (p. 196).

poetry which in general was intended (like that of Golden-Age Spain) for performance, with a stress on its auditory qualities. Probably particular metres, like the musical modes, were expected to have specific psychological effects; they might at times be chosen, and changed, to intensify the expression of emotion, to condition the audience's experience of emotions, or to evoke emotional associations.[26]

The *comedia* is thus not alone, though it is outstanding, in the flexibility of its form; we who admire it should not apologize for but advertise this aspect of its uniqueness.

If we review Morley's attempts to explain *why* Spanish dramatists 'indulged a lyric bent by writing whole plays, romantic or realistic, in short meters invented for and best employed in lyrics', we may not agree that this was 'one manifestation of the lack of *mesura* so characteristic of much of Spanish literature and Spanish history ... one phase of Spanish lack of taste'.[27] We may be happier with his suggestion that the imagination of Golden-Age playwrights was positively stimulated, as was Bretón's, by the technical difficulty of composing dramatic dialogue in short lines, heavily rhymed—not to mention the range of expressive variation which was afforded them by the different strophes. We may be happiest to attribute the metrical structure of the *comedia*, 'combinación de todos los modos líricos conocidos entonces'[28] to the poetic virtuosity of its creator, Lope de Vega, who was after all 'el mejor lírico para sus contemporáneos'. Lope may in one way or another have been anticipated by Gil Vicente, Juan de la Cueva or Cristóbal de Virués; but metrical variety, like so much else in Golden-Age drama, was not so much invented as established as the norm when he 'alzóse con la monarquía cómica'. To quote Courtney Bruerton: 'por lo menos hasta el año 1611, el genio fecundo de Lope encabezó no sólo la evolución del género, sino también de su versificación.'[29]

[26] See W.B. Stanford, *Greek Tragedy and the Emotions: an Introductory Study* (London, 1983), pp. 49-75, which the author generously allowed me to see in typescript.

[27] Morley, 'The Curious Phenomenon...', p. 462.

[28] Montesinos, p. 13.

[29] Courtney Bruerton, 'La versificación dramática española en el período 1587-1610', *NRFH*, 10 (1956), 337-64 (p. 364).

His eight lines in the *Arte nuevo* (305-12) are the most significant and specific discussion of the subject in the Golden Age. There is far less substance in the recommendations—mostly in favor of *redondillas*—by Francisco Cascales, Suárez de Figueroa or even Carlos Boyl; the versification the latter recommends in *A un licenciado que deseaba hacer comedias* may reflect his own practice, but as Morel-Fatio observed is 'notamment plus pauvre que celle de l'*Arte* de Lope'.[30] 305 and 306 are the really revolutionary—or reactionary—lines, in that they categorically advocate, or rather codify, the extension to versification of the classical principle of *decorum* or appropriateness (adumbrated, for instance, as we have seen, by López Pinciano):

> Acomode los versos con prudencia
> a los sujetos de que va tratando.

The remainder, though full of intriguing insights, are important chiefly in that they specifically instance as many as six strophic forms, with possible functions. They are far too frequently quoted as if they constituted a considered statement and a system; admirers endeavour to show that they were or should have been remembered and rigidly obeyed or only minimally modified by others, detractors that they were unsuitable as 'las reglas que se supone hay para nuestra poesía dramática' and did not closely correspond to Lope's own habits of composition before or after 1609. Morley and Bruerton were rightly taken to task by C.E. Anibal for having come 'dangerously near fallacious interpretation of his imprecision there as a lack of fundamental principles'. Lope was too spontaneous and intuitive an artist ever to have seriously enunciated—let alone to have doggedly followed—a rigid set of rules, but 'within reasonably elastic bounds Lope was very consistent in his method of selecting the particular verse-form that he felt would most fittingly create or sustain the dominant mood each scene required'. Whatever his

---

[30] Morel-Fatio, 'Les défenseurs de la comedia', *BH*, 4 (1902), 30-62 (p. 54). For more recent commentaries on the *Arte nuevo*, see the edition by Juana de José Prades (Madrid, 1971) and Juan Manuel Rozas, *Significado y doctrina del 'Arte nuevo' de Lope de Vega* (Madrid, 1976).

faults, he was 'an undisputed master of those colorful details that create atmosphere. His kaleidoscopic manipulation of verse-forms must be recognized as of primary importance among such intangibles. The role they play...may well lie beyond our perfect comprehension, but the pace and mood set by his metrics certainly contributes a potent and to some extent an appreciable influence.'[31]

The same may be said of course, in different degrees, of all competent writers of *comedias*. We are still a long way, despite anything we have learned in the intervening forty years, from 'perfect comprehension'—which the writers themselves no doubt frequently lacked—of their reasons for preferring particular metres at particular moments. But for any able and sensitive artist the use of one rather than another, we may be confident, must have related to the theme, source or setting of the action; the rank, personality or state of mind of the characters; the mood, intensity or tempo of an episode; and that episode's role in the development of the plot: its exposition, elaboration, elucidation or resolution. We can discern habits and conventions peculiar to one author or common to many, so that often we may feel confident that we can understand a writer's choices and even question their correctness. Yet there is still ample room for healthy disagreement amongst us; indeed this is one of the aspects of the *comedia* most open to and in need of interpretation. As editors, therefore, we should make our readers conscious of the complexities; we should encourage them to 'auralise' the varying verse forms in which our text was written, and to assess their impact in the theatre as it must have been assessed, in the seventeenth century, by perceptive *oyentes*.

It might be objected that such *oyentes* are likely to have been unaware of the metrical forms they were hearing. John G. Weiger has suggested for instance that 'el público no suele contar ni sílabas ni versos al escuchar una comedia, si bien los cuenta el poeta al componer su obra'.[32] Even if this were true, we should be interested in how the author modified his metrics to achieve his effects without his audience understanding the mechanics. But in

---

[31] Claude E. Anibal, review of S.G. Morley and C. Bruerton, *The Chronology of Lope de Vega's Comedias* (New York, 1940), in *HR*, 11 (1943), 338-53.
[32] Weiger, p. 39.

any case I cannot be alone in expecting, in a performance of Shakespeare, to be able to identify each and every iambic pentameter, in admiring most those modern actors—Olivier, for instance—who can keep the verse form clear as well as impersonating and 'emoting', and in feeling impatient with those who lack the technique and sensitivty to do so. It seems probably that Golden-Age performers were able, as Bertram Joseph has said the Elizabethans were, 'to create character and express emotion so that they seemed to be presenting on the stage real people behavingly truthfully under the stress of their feelings; yet the verse was also spoken as verse should be spoken'.[33] The more educated members of their varied audience, moreover, were accustomed, outside the *corral*, if not to writing verse to reading it (or hearing it read) aloud. Such 'doctos y cortesanos' may of course have been outnumbered, then as now, as Lope laments in the *Prólogo dialogístico*: 'pues nadie se podra persuadir con mediano entendimiento que la mayor parte de la mugeres que aquel jaulon encierra, y de los ignorantes que assiten a los bancos, entienden los versos, las figuras retoricas, los concetos y sentencias, las imitaciones, y el grave o comun estilo'.[34] As Montesinos commented on this passage: 'Se nos hace difícil...imaginar que un público de mosqueteros y mujercillas notase siquiera la diversidad de metros y el porqué de su empleo. En este aspecto, la comedia iba ciertamente dirigida a los que pudieran apreciar y agradecer los "estudios" del autor'.[35] But even the illiterate groundlings, tolerant at least as they must have been of the other literary elements Lope mentions, may have had some inkling of poetic form. As an anonymous *loa* of 1609 informs us (though perhaps ironically): 'Todos gustan de concepto; / Ya no hay vulgo, nadie ignora; / todos quieren en la farsa / buenos versos, trazas proprias'.[36]

There is in fact evidence that dramatists supposed that spectators would expect and recognize particular verse-forms (sometimes signalled by conventional formulae) in particular

---

[33] Bertram Joseph, *The Tragic Actor* (London, 1959), pp. XI-XII.
[34] Lope de Vega, *Decimasexta parte de las comedias* (Madrid, 1621), fol. ¶¶ recto.
[35] Montesinos, p. 13.
[36] Quoted by Frenk, p. 121.

dramatic contexts—and notice if those expectations were not fulfilled. When in Calderón's *Casa con dos puertas*, Act I, Don Félix and Lisardo meet, and Don Félix says 'Escuchadme', Calabazas predicts 'dos larguísimos romances'; in fact we get 248 lines of *romance* from one, though a mere 26 from the other. At the beginning of Lope's *La noche de San Juan,* Leonor tells Inés that she will have to describe her situation in a long *romance*; shall she say 'aquello de *escucha*'? No, says Inés, 'porque si te escucho yo,/ necio advertimiento es'. In Act I of *El saber puede dañar*, Turín confesses aside that when his master Carlos said 'Escucha', he feared a long narrative monologue in that same metre: 'Salí de notable trance,/ que cuando el *escucha* oí/ de dos leguas presumí/ que teníamos romance'. In Act I of *Amor con vista*, Tomé admits that he had assumed, mistakenly, that the explanatory monologue which Fenis has just delivered—in eighteen six-line *liras*—would be in *romances*: '¡Vive Dios que me has cogido!/ Gusto de señora tienes,/ que yo esperaba un romance,/ y en verso grave procedes.'[37]

In *La victoria de la honra* Lope, sent by Antonio to follow Leonor, tells his master as he exits: 'Dile entretanto un soneto', and Antonio does so. Similarly, in *Pobreza no es vileza* Panduro, left alone on stage, remarks: 'Solo he quedado. ¿Qué haré?/ Quiero decir un soneto', and does. In *El desdén vengado* Tomín, after Feniso has entered, spoken fourteen lines and left, comments: 'Sin duda venía/ a decir este soneto'. And in Calderón's *Gustos y disgustos*...the *dueña* Leonor, entering an empty stage, says she will have to recite a soliloquy or a sonnet, chooses a soliloquy and continues in *redondillas*.[38]

How in practice should we be influenced, as editors, by the considerations I have outlined? In the first place, our decision to edit a particular play may have to do with its versification. Scansion, rhyme and above all metrical structure have provided the most important 'objective criteria', other than external evidence, which scholars have so far attempted to use to determine

---

[37] B.A.E. 7, 130b; Ac.N. 8, 133; B.A.E. 41, 116c; Ac.N.10, 605.
[38] Ac.N. 10, 415; Ac.N. 12, 500; Ac. 15, 401; B.A.E. 12, 3c.

authorship and date of composition.[39] Our inclination to tackle, say, *El condenado por desconfiado* or *La estrella de Sevilla*, may therefore be weakened or strengthened by such evidence, and we shall at least need to discuss it in our introduction. Concern to probe such problems may even account in part for our interest in the play; this was clearly the case with *Fernán Méndez Pinto*, as edited by Cohen, Rogers and Rose, or with *Don Domingo de don Blas*, as edited by Vern G. Williamsen. My own edition of *El sufrimiento premiado* was motivated not solely by the play's intrinsic merits but by a desire to determine whether a work only ever published as by Juan Pérez de Montalbán was written, as seems likely, by Lope de Vega, perhaps when Montalbán was in his cradle. All these may be offered as examples of 'attribution-by-edition'; and in each case the versification of the play had an important role in the argument.[40]

Having chosen our play, we shall normally choose our base-text, assuming that the autograph is not extant, on external evidence; but versification will sometimes offer an additional guide. The most correct, complete and complex text, from the point of view of its verse, is likely to be the nearest to what its author originally wrote. For instance, the second Madrid edition of Lope's *Sexta parte* (1616) was based, in respect of *some* of its plays, on better texts than the first (1615); faulty rhymes and missing lines help us to say which. Later texts, on the other hand, may have been tidied up; we must be on our guard. Vera Tassis, for example, regularised (and often 'improved') the plays of Calderón when he printed them; and the earliest *suelta* of *El condenado por*

[39] See S.G. Morley, '*Objective Criteria for Judging Authorship and Chronology in the Comedia*', *HR*, 5 (1937), 280-85. On verse forms and their occurrence in the work of individual authors, see the excellent bibliographies in S.G. Morley and C. Bruerton, *Cronología de las comedias de Lope de Vega* (Madrid, 1968), and in Diego Marín, *Uso y función...* (note 57 below), and add: Vern G. Williamsen, 'The Versification of Antonio Mira de Amescua's *Comedias* and of some *Comedias* attributed to him', in *Studies in Honor of Ruth Lee Kennedy*, edited by Williamsen and A.F. Michael Atlee (Chapel Hill, 1977), 151-67.

[40] *Fernán Méndez Pinto*, edited by Louise G. Cohen, Francis M. Rogers and Constance H. Rose (Harvard, 1974); Juan Ruiz de Alarcón, *Don Domingo de Don Blas*, edited by Vern G. Williamsen (Valencia, 1975); *El sufrimiento premiado, comedia...atribuida...a Lope de Vega Carpio*, edited by Victor Dixon (London, 1967).

desconfiado, though its text is probably a cut version of that in Tirso's *Segunda parte*, has numerous variants which 'consist of slight differences in wording to make the metre right'.[41] Thus at line 1663, where at least three lines of a *quintilla* are missing, with a clear gap in the sense, three lines are supplied in the *suelta*, much as three very different lines, two centuries later, were to be supplied by Hartzenbusch. Only obvious *errata* or *lacunae*, however, were usually corrected like this, and later texts usually contain new metrical irregularities. Again, rehashes by inferior authors which modify the versification will generally be shorter and simpler; thus the *sueltas* of *El perro del hortelano* lack 198 lines of Lope's third act, but 160 of these (146 *sueltas* and a sonnet) have been replaced by 87 *romances*, and another sonnet by a *redondilla*.

In attempting to establish our 'ideal version', it is important that we be familiar with our author's practices as a poet, for with these, we are bound to suppose (although, as autographs tell us, few writers are wholly consistent), his original must have agreed. We should be aware, in examining our base-text and collating it with others, of lines apparently missing from or superfluous to a strophe; of lines irregularly stressed, or containing too few or too many syllables, in view of our author's habits in respect of syneresis and hiatus, synalepha and azeuxis;[42] and of irregularities of rhyme and assonance (Andalusian rhymes, inadmissible auto-rhymes, assonance instead of consonance and vice-versa, assonance between adjacent rhymes...).[43] Any discrepancy from

---

[41] Tirso de Molina, *El condenado por desconfiado*, edited by Daniel Rogers (Oxford, 1974); further references are to this edition.

[42] On the practice of individual authors, see especially: Walter Poesse, *The Internal Line-Structure of Thirty Autograph Plays of Lope de Vega* (Bloomington, 1949); G.E. Wade, 'The Orthoëpy of the Holographic *Comedias* of Vélez de Guevara', *HR*, 9 (1941), 459-81; W.E. Wilson, 'The Orthoëpy of Certain Words in the Plays of Guillén de Castro', *HR*, 21 (1953), 146-50.

[43] On rhyme in the *comedia*, see the studies by J.H. Arjona: 'The Use of Autorhymes in the XVIIth-Century *Comedia*', *HR*, 21 (1953), 273-301; 'Defective Rhymes and Rhyming Techniques in Lope de Vega's Autograph *Comedias*', *HR*, 23 (1955), 1082-8; 'False Andalusian Rhymes in Lope de Vega and their Bearing on the Authorship of Doubtful *Comedias*', *HR*, 24 (1956), 290-305; 'Improper Use of Consonantal Rhyme in Lope de Vega and its Significance Concerning the Authorship of Doubtful Plays', *Hispanófila* No. 16 (1962), 7-39; also Manuel Ascarza, 'The Mixture of Assonant and Consonantal Rhyme in Lope's Theater', *HR*, 48 (1980), 111-17.

his normal usage should cause us to suspect a corruption, which we should if possible remedy (by recourse to other texts, to other editors, or to our own ingenuity) in either our text or our notes, giving proper account, in either case, of the rival readings.

It may thus be possible, occasionally, to supply whole lines which are missing in the base-text. Early in Act III of *El condenado por desconfiado,* the *Segunda parte*'s text lacks a line which should rhyme with Celia's 'y poneos bien con Dios' (2134); the *sueltas* supply 'que habéis de morir los dos', but Hartzenbusch: 'que es lo que os importa a vos'. Similarly, we have Hartzenbusch to thank for the 'convincing reconstruction' of line 2494: 'escupir el hombre al cielo'. Advisedly, I think, Daniel Rogers included this line, between square brackets, in his text, since it is essential to the sense, but gave the alternative versions of 2135, which is not, only in an end-note.

Without such help, a twentieth-century editor will usually be chary of trying to repair omissions; but he must be conscious of and draw attention to them. He should note, for instance, in editing *El villano en su rincón,* that in Juan Labrador's famous soliloquy lines 1-3 or 4-6 of the fourth stanza are missing, and suspect that his famous epitaph should include a line to rhyme with its third, 'ni vio la Corte ni al Rey'. He should also suspect, by contrast, that line 2644: 'Mal mi gusto persuadís' (which turns a *redondilla* into an odd *quintilla*) may perhaps be an interpolation;[44] but he should recognize lines 514-26 as that regular irregularity, a *décima larga* amid a laisse of *décimas.*[45]

Our base-text will certainly contain short lines, which cry out to be lengthened; again we must look for help, and exercise judgment. Thus in *El condenado,* at line 274, the *Segunda parte* text has: 'lo que le he de preguntar/ cuando le llegue a ver'; it seems likely that the earliest *suelta* was correct in supplying *yo* before *le llegue.* On the other hand, when at line 1362 we find the 'hendecasyllable': 'Perdonad, padre de mis ojos' we may not be convinced by the *mío* which Hartzenbusch inserted after *padre.*

---

[44] Note, however, the stray *quintilla* in *El condenado por desconfiado* (329-33), and see Vern G. Williamsen, 'Some Odd *Quintillas* and a Question of Authenticity in Tirso's Theatre', *RF* 82 (1970), 488-512.

[45] See especially Morley and Bruerton, *Cronología,* p. 38.

The overlong lines in our base-text, by contrast, will call out to be shortened. Thus the *princeps* of *El perro del hortelano*, at line 214, has: '¿Para qué me niegas lo menos?'; we might be tempted to read '¿Por qué...?', but an early MS and the second edition, independently, tell us rather to leave out the *me*. Line 2506 is more intriguing. Two copies of the *princeps* have: 'A casa voy, que no está de aquí muy lejos'; another copy, and the second edition, omit the *no*, making just as much sense and a proper line. But since preferring this reading I have wondered whether Lope may have written the *no*, but not the *que*. Eight lines later, we find in the *princeps* (I transcribe exactly): 'pues oy de aquel amor se hallò tan nueua,/ que a penas juraràs que me conoce'. In this case the lines are metrically unexceptionable; in fact one must resist on grounds of scansion Ramón Rozzell's plausible emendation to *juraras*.[46] Lope never wrote, surely, a hendecasyllable with a major stress on syllable five.

Faulty rhymes are often corruptions, quickly corrected. In *El sufrimiento premiado*, for instance, I was able readily to resolve six obvious misprints in the only two printed editions. In *El amor enamorado*, lines 2271-74, we can be confident that Venus, who is addressing Sirena, calls her by her name rather than 'Señora', so that there is no lack of rhyme with 'buena'.[47] We must, however, be aware of (and of course not seek to 'correct') what may merely appear to be faults of rhyme. We (and our readers) need to know for example whether a particular auto-rhyme falls inside or outside the surprisingly wide range accepted by contemporary practice (and even theory). Again, both must be conscious of those kinds of rhyme which would seem incorrect today but were correct at the time—like, for instance, *perfeto-conceto* in lines 8-9 of *El caballero de Olmedo*: these may be obscured by the spelling of our base-text, which our editing policy may or may not allow us to modify.

In the way we present the text to our readers, on the printed page, we should seek to keep before their minds the fact that it is a play to be performed, but simultaneously to promote their

---

[46] Review of the edition by Eugène Kohler (Paris, 1951), *HR*, 21 (1953), 164-69.
[47] Lope de Vega, *El amor enamorado*, edited by John B. Wooldridge, Jr. (Madrid, 1978).

awareness of its sound and structure as a dramatic poem. They should read it, that is, both as a script and as a species of score. To quote Montesinos again: 'La comedia está concebida de un modo, podríamos decir, musical, en que cada escena tiene una tonalidad determinada, según su índole'.[48]

It may be helpful, however, to define what he meant here— or should, perhaps, have meant—by 'cada escena'. He did *not* mean, one trusts, those false divisions devised by eighteenth- and nineteenth-century editors (and their twentieth-century survivors) who clutter the text with 'ESCENA XXVI' or the like whenever a character enters or exits. The only practical purpose of such interpolations—ease of reference—is far better served by numbering every fifth line of the play, from start to finish, and they positively conceal its actual structure. Every standard *comedia* is in three acts, but each of these consists, primarily, of a series of what are sometimes called *cuadros* but I would prefer to refer to as *salidas*. (I think of José Pellicer: 'Cada Jornada debe constar de tres *scenas*, que vulgarmente se dizen *salidas*').[49] The end of each *salida* was signalled to the spectators by the conventional device of emptying the stage; the appearance of different performers was the cue to expect—as we would today after a blackout or crossfade—a change in the time and/or location of the action, the nature of which would have to be inferred from the costumes and dialogue.[50] Lope de Vega, in his autographs, normally indicated such 'natural breaks'—no doubt because each *salida* was for him a unit of poetic composition—by a line across the page ending in a rubric, and it will be helpful to our readers if we imitate this habit—as Tamesis Texts have done so far—whenever we edit a *comedia*.

The author would start each new *salida*—with rare exceptions—in a new verse form. But within the *salida* he would often change metres again, *not* (unless coincidentally) at the entry

---

[48] Montesinos, p. 13.

[49] 'Idea de la comedia de Castilla...', in *Lágrimas panegíricas a la temprana muerte del Doctor Juan Pérez de Montalbán. Recogidas por Pedro Grande de Tena* (Madrid, 1639), fol. 151 recto. In practice the number of *salidas* was hardly ever so regular as Pellicer proposed, though there was an overall tendency to reduce and standardize; thus *Peribáñez* has 5:7:7, *La vida es sueño*, 2:2:3.

[50] Of course characters and action may be supposed to move, gradually, within a single *salida*, as in at least the first 680 lines of *El alcalde de Zalamea*.

or exit of a character, but to modify significantly, as we have seen, the aural impact of the verse. The successive passages in different metres and stanza forms are indeed, I submit, the true *(sub)-escenas, micro-secuencias* or building-blocks of the play; the poetic structure of a *comedia* coincides with, *is* its dramatic structure, and to clarify one can only illuminate the other.

To return to the analogy with music, each *salida* can be compared to a movement or number, each change of metrical form to a change of key-signature or a new indication of tempo or expression. I propose, therefore, that in future we all adopt a novel but simple convention; that we label each change of '*tonalidad*' by inserting in the margin the name of every new metre—not merely to alert the reader to the change but to invite him, implicitly, to consider its significance.

Every such change of metre should surely be signalled, in any case, by leaving at least a single line-space before it, even when—as very occasionally happens—it occurs in mid-sentence; there is something indeed to be said for inserting such a space before each stanza of a laisse, although this might be felt to disrupt the flow of dialogue, especially in *redondillas*. I recall only one edition in which such a layout was used, that of Mira's *La segunda de don Álvaro* by Nellic Sánchez-Arce (Mexico 1960). The normal practice at present is merely to indent the first line of every stanza (including *tercetos*); this convention should be followed too for the fifth, ninth and twelfth lines of sonnets, and extended perhaps to the fifth line of *décimas*—after, that is, the usual pause at the end of the fourth.

A missing line (if not supplied, conjecturally, between square brackets) should be represented by a row of dots; two or more, I suggest, by two rows. Such omissions, moreover, should be counted in the numbering of lines as if the stanza were complete, as beyond doubt it almost always originally was; what we cannot know, or allow for, is the number of whole stanzas which may have been lost. Lines of verse meant to be sung should also be included in the numbering (except when a song is merely referred to by its first line); but passages in prose (e.g. letters) should not be numbered.

Italics are a convenient device for clarifying poetic structure.

They should be used for all refrains, and for lines repeated as a motif; for the *texto* of a gloss, and for its lines when they appear at the ends of stanzas;[51] and probably for poetic allusions—in *Los cabellos de Absalón*, for example, for *O dulces prendas, por mi bien halladas* and for *Salid sin duelo, lágrimas, corriendo*, and perhaps even, in *La vida es sueño*, for *Y los sueños, sueños son*—with a note to refer to the source. Italics should likewise be used for the lyrics of songs sung on- or off-stage, and probably indeed to distinguish everything sung from the spoken dialogue; in reviewing, for instance, the superb edition by Varey, Shergold and Sage of Luis Vélez's *zarzuela, Los celos hacen estrellas*, I suggested that this might have been done for the twenty per cent of the text which was to be sung.[52]

What should we include in our introduction to the text in respect of its versification? As J.G. Weiger has noted: 'Es habitual presentar el esquema métrico de una comedia aunque no siempre encontramos un intento de ver en la versificación algo vinculado a la acción dramática'.[53] Indeed in some otherwise excellent introductions—in Peter Dunn's *El alcalde de Zalamea*, for instance, or Alan Paterson's *La venganza de Tamar*—one is surprised to find no reference at all to the metrical structure.

We should certainly list the metres in sequence, act by act, giving the line-numbers of each passage, and the number of lines. We should indicate here the assonating vowels in passages of *romance*,[54] the types of *quintilla, silva* and sonnet used, and the proportion of *pareados* in passages of *sueltos*; and of course we should point out any pecularities of form. For each act, we should indicate the total number of passages; for each metre, the number of passages, the total number of lines, and the percentage of the play as a whole which that total represents. We may or may not wish to

[51] On glosses in the *comedia*, see H. Janner, 'La glosa española. Estudio histórico de su métrica y de sus temas', *RFE*, 27 (1943), 181-232.

[52] Luis Vélez de Guevara, *Los celos hacen estrellas,* edited by J.E. Varey and N.D. Shergold, with an edition and study of the music by Jack Sage (London, 1970); reviewed *HR*, 42 (1974), 101-03.

[53] Guillén de Castro, *Las hazañas del Cid*, edited by John H. Weiger (Madrid, 1980), p. 27.

[54] We need not, I think, emulate R.W. Tyler, who in his edition of Lope de Vega, *La corona de Hungría* (Chapel Hill, 1972), pp. 62-64, listed the 511 words used for *romance* assonances.

compare the proportion of Castilian to Italianate lines, or to compare the figures for one version of our play with those for another.[55]

Merely to record such 'raw data', however, is to ignore those aesthetic questions which we and our readers ought to be asking. The real point of our having 'tabulated meter changes scene by scene', was, in Anibal's words, 'so that the precise succession of strophic forms, and consequently the rise and fall of the dramatic action, could be more clearly appreciated...For true metrical perspective this must somewhere be done for each play'.[56] In fact studies of the 'use and function' of polymetric verse in the *comedia* have been of three main types:

1) the pioneering study by Diego Marín of 27 plays by Lope (at once a large and a small number), and a few later *estudios de conjunto*;[57]

2) a few short studies of individual authors and plays in which the subject has been a central or incidental concern;[58] and

3) a considerable number of critical editions in which it has been more or less deeply discussed. Very possibly, indeed, while we await the undertaking of a truly comprehensive study, our understanding of the subject may best be advanced by the analysis of individual *comedias*, and every editor and reader could and should contribute his widow's mite simply by asking at each

[55] Thus in both *Carlos V en Francia*, edited by A.G. Reichenberger (Philadelphia, 1962), and *El primero Benavides*, edited by Reichenberger and Augusta Espantoso Foley (Philadelphia, 1973), the versification of Lope's autograph is compared with that of the *Parte* text.

[56] Anibal, p. 342.

[57] Diego Marín, *Uso y función de la versificación dramática en Lope de Vega* (Valencia, 1962). Two important recent studies are; Vern G. Williamsen, 'La función estructural del verso en la comedia del siglo de oro', *Actas del V Congreso Internacional de Hispanistas* (Bordeaux, 1977), pp. 883-91, slightly expanded as 'The Structural Function of Polymetry in the Spanish *Comedia*', in *Perspectivas de la comedia*, edited by A.V. Ebersole (Chapel Hill, 1978), pp. 33-47; Jan Bakker, 'Versificación y estructura de la comedia de Lope', in *Diálogos hispánicos de Amsterdam No. 2* (Amsterdam, 1981), pp. 93-101.

[58] See especially Peter N. Dunn, 'Some Uses of Sonnets in the Plays of Lope de Vega', *BHS* 34 (1957), 213-22; Victor Dixon, '*El castigo sin venganza*: the Artistry of Lope de Vega', in *Studies...Wilson* (see note 15), pp. 63-81; Jack Sage, Critical Guide to Lope de Vega, *El caballero de Olmedo* (London, 1974), pp. 74-80; Michael McGaha, 'The Structure of *El caballero de Olmedo*', *Hispania*, 61 (1978), 451-58; Pablo Cabañas, 'Función dramática de dos sonetos de Mira de Amescua', *BRAE*, 56 (1976), 147-59.

metre-change: Why? or With what effect?

Some editors offer a synopsis of the action which summarizes its content laisse by laisse, often with comments *en passant* on the suitability of the successive forms.[59] This device I must commend because it acknowledges, implicitly, the coincidence of metrical and dramatic structures on which I have insisted; but some aspects of 'use and function' are not amenable to this treatment, and one grudges wasting space, which is invariably at a premium, on a 'spoon-feeding' summary of the plot. There are essentially two alternative approaches: to discuss the use of each verse form in the course of the play as a whole, or to consider, as I have suggested, each change of metre, sequentially— with reference of course, in either case, to what is known of the habits of the author and of his contemporaries.

Some editors use all three methods, and therefore offer an admirably comprehensive treatment of the question; such are Arnold Reichenberger, in his edition of *Carlos V en Francia*, and (with A. Espantoso Foley) of *El primero Benavides*, and Diego Marín, in his editions of *La dama boba* and (with Evelyn Rugg) of *El galán de la Membrilla*. These last two, popular and academic editions respectively, should be our models, although most of us will feel constrained to devote less space to the subject.[60] In my own 'college' edition of *El perro del hortelano*, I attempted to analyze its metrical structure (as well as to discuss polymetry in general and to teach my readers to count syllables and recognize

---

[59] See Luis Vélez de Guevara, *La niña de Gómez Arias*, edited by Ramón Rozzell (Granada, 1959); Lope de Vega, *El galán de la Membrilla,* edited by Diego Marín and Evelyn Rugg (Madrid, 1962); *Carlos V en Francia*; Lope de Vega, *El príncipe inocente*, and *El amor desatinado*, both edited by Justo García Morales (Madrid, 1964 and 1968); Lope de Vega, *Las almenas de Toro*, edited by Thomas E. Case (Chapel Hill, 1971); *El primero Benavides*; Lope de Vega, *La dama boba*, edited by Diego Marín (Madrid, 1976).

[60] Other editions—not an exhaustive list—in which 'use and function' has been discussed in some detail include: *La niña de Gómez Arias; La segunda de Don Álvaro*: Calderón, *La vida es sueño*, edited by A.E. Sloman (Manchester, 1961); *Carlos V en Francia*; *El primero Benavides*; Calderón, *El postrer duelo de España*, edited by Guy Rossetti (London, 1977); *Las hazañas del Cid*. One can only sympathize with the brave attempt by Luciano García Lorenzo, in his edition of Guillén de Castro, *Los mal casados de Valencia* (Madrid, 1976), p. 41, to represent as one of the play's 'indudables valores' the fact that it is wholly in *redondillas*: 'Ni reflexivos sonetos, ni quejosas décimas; breve y fluida estrofa y verso octosílabo, el verso hispano por excelencia'.

forms) in some six pages, or about one-tenth of the introduction. That seems to me about the right proportion; metrical structure must compete for our attention with other aspects of the *comedia*. But it must not be neglected. To quote yet again, and yet again to take issue with a great scholar: 'The extraordinary variety of meters employed in the *comedia* surpassed anything known in any other drama of the world. From two to a dozen, and even more may be used. Most of them were originally developed as lyric forms, and many critics believe that such variety is an obstacle to the fullest dramatic effect'.[61] Some of us believe that that variety, and that lyrical quality—both gloriously exemplified, for instance, in *El caballero de Olmedo* or *La vida es sueño*—are not only distinctive attributes but cherished strengths of a genre we admire, but would hope eventually to understand rather better.

---

[61] S.G. Morley, 'Objective criteria...', p. 283.

A COMMENTARY ON 'THE USES OF POLYMETRY' AND THE EDITING OF THE MULTI-STROPHIC TEXTS OF THE SPANISH *COMEDIA*

Vern G. Williamsen

The lucid, measured views of Victor Dixon expressed in the preceding essay go a long way toward explaining: (1) the poetic reasons behind the multi-strophic texts that are typical of the *comedia*, (2) the uses to which a knowledge of Spanish versification may be put as an aid in making editorial decisions, and (3) the critical purposes that may be served by a thorough understanding of the principles involved. After careful consideration of what Dixon has had to say on the subject, I am convinced that there is a need to underscore—by means of examples—some of the points he has so cogently set forth and to expand upon others of them as a guide to those who may be in the process of editing a *comedia* text, thinking of doing so, or judging an edition already prepared.

Because the use of multiple strophes by playwrights of the Golden Age *comedia* seems to have followed some formulaic pattern or patterns that had the effect of communicating specific qualities of that text to the audience of its time, it might be well to study the semiotic nature of the system. Obviously, the poets of the *comedia* would not have adhered to the system so closely if, indeed, it had not served just such a communicative, supra-verbal function. I do not care to enter here upon the question of whether or not such was the conscious intent of the author or whether the audiences were entirely aware of the process. For our purposes it is enough that the polymetry involved did serve as an informative signal, either intuitive or deliberate, in the progress of the work as it moved from the poet's pen to the participating public on either a conscious or a subliminal level.

All of this only makes our work as editors and critics more difficult because we, in our own times, do not yet understand the vagaries of the poetic principles involved more than partially. Alexander A. Parker once said, "The Spanish drama of the Golden Age speaks a language of its own which we must first learn before we can properly understand what it says."[1] As Victor Dixon has pointed out, some beginning steps have been taken in the direction of learning the rules—the grammar—involved in comprehending that language.[2] Here I would like to add my plea for an intelligent and thorough study of the versification of each play as scholarly editions of them are prepared, since it is only through the gradual accumulation of numerous such elements that sufficient data may eventually become available to the future scholar wanting to codify the system as a whole.

1. Alexander A. Parker, *The Approach to the Spanish Drama of the Golden Age* (London, 1957), p. 27.

2. To the list of items that Victor Dixon has placed in his paper on sources of information dealing with dramatic versification (with an appeal to make further reference to the bibliographies provided in them), I would like to add that there are many manuals dealing with the techniques involved. I have found most helpful to me Tomás Navarro Tomás, *Métrica española* (Syracuse, 1956). Too recent to have been included in Dixon's note is the publication of a study by Diego Marín, "Función dramática de la versificación en el teatro de Calderón," *Segismundo*, 16 (1982). Nor should the editor forget such basic sources of information about Golden Age versification as Díaz Rengifo's *Arte poética* (originally 1592), Carballo's *El cisne de Apolo* (1602), and other such books on poetic theory written during the period of the *comedia*. A good standard anthology of such texts is the *Preceptiva dramática española*, eds. Alberto Porqueras Mayo and Federico Sánchez Escribano (Madrid, 1972).

Dixon has quite properly and thoroughly exposed the importance of the aural qualities of the *comedia*, its reliance on poetic tradition as a source for poetic content, the use of varied strophic forms as a signal for change in mood (tonality) or structure, the question of decorum, and the traditionally recognized relationships between strophic form and theme. He has also disposed of the question of the ways in which various individuals in the audience may have responded quite differently to metric changes depending upon their relative sophistication in matters poetic. At this point I would like to add a few comments pointing to new directions in which recent research has been heading, not in order to supply an hypothesized codification for which we do not yet have sufficient data, but as an aid to editors of *comedia* texts in order to indicate additional matters that may be of concern to them as they approach the texts they are working with and are preparing to write the needed introductory studies.

Besides the purposes served by a strophic form as audible signals underscoring impending dramatic changes or structural elements of the drama being performed as discussed by Dixon, I have recently shown that the playwrights made use of the basic qualities of poetic form (rhyme, rhythm, and rhetoric) to heighten the dramatic effort of key scenes.[3] They did this by carefully choosing the rhyming words, as those most likely to stand forth with special vigor as the actor spoke the lines, to emphasize the central theme, action, or dramatic intent of the scene in which they fall. In addition, there are examples of deliberate use of the varied rhythmic patterns and the rhetorical structures peculiar to poetic discourse to the same effect. Most often these devices were used as the poet had recourse to an unusual or less frequently employed strophic form.[4] A few quotations from several plays chosen to

3. Vern G. Williamsen, "Rhyme as a Form of Audible 'Sign' in Two Calderonian Plays," *Neophilologus*, 68 (1984), 546-56.

4. The editor must certainly look with a careful eye at any strophic form that breaks the general pattern of textual presentation. Early in the development of the *comedia*, the *redondilla* and *quintilla* seem to have been used for the basic action of the plays; by the turn of the century, poets seemed to have gone almost exclusively over to the *redondilla* and to have used the *quintilla* only for the sake of variety. Clearly, any use of the *romance* during this period would merit scrutiny to identify the reason for its use and the poetic effect it may have had. As the century progressed, the *romance* tended to replace the *redondilla* as the

exemplify the several processes just described should serve to clarify the point and to be a guide on the subject for an editor of *comedias* who, in addition to the principles set forth in Victor Dixon's essay, must keep them in mind as the text is prepared and the introductory discussion of the play is prepared.

In Guillén de Castro's *Las mocedades del Cid*, the turning point in the structure of the play is certainly the scene in the middle of the second act in which Rodrigo comes to Jimena's apartments, after having killed her father in a duel for the sake of honor, to offer her his own life in return.[5] The key points in this scene lie in the fact that the two are caught on the opposing horns of the dilemma posed by love and honor. She could not love him if his honor were lost, yet to retain it he was forced into a duel with her father. She, too, is impelled by her own honor to seek vengeance for her father's death. But the two are in love, each—in neo-Platonic fashion—desiring only the well being of the other. Castro sets this scene in a strophic form quite unusual for the seventeenth-century *comedia*: a strophe that, although heavily used by the playwrights of the early sixteenth century, had all but disappeared from the poetic lexicon of later writers. The form is that of alternating *redondillas* and *quintillas* with a *quebrado* in the third verse of the *quintilla* (ABBA:CDdCD). The short time span separating the rhyme *D* from its reappearance in the shortened, four-syllable *quebrado* (*d*) has the effect of audibly enhancing the third appearance of the consonant rhyme (*D*) in the last verse of each *copla*. Even a cursory reading of some sample *coplas* from the passage will demonstrate the effect clearly.

> RODRIGO: Tu padre el Conde, Lozano
> en el nombre y en el brío
> puso en las canas del mío
> la atrevida injusta mano;

basic verse form in the *comedia*, and, as Diego Marín has shown, the *quintilla* that had nearly disappeared from the poetic lexicon in the 1620's reappeared to be used especially in scenes of dramatic tension in plays written in later decades. All other strophic forms seem to have been used in some way as signals of change in structure, tone, or action.

5. Guillén de Castro, *Las mocedades del Cid*, ed. G.W. Umphrey (New York, 1939). All textual references to the play are to this edition.

y aunque me vi sin honor,
se malogró mi esperanza
en tal mudanza,
con tal fuerza, que tu amor
puso en duda mi *venganza*.
   Mas en tan gran desventura
lucharon a mi despecho,
contrapuestos en mi pecho
mi afrenta con tu hermosura;
   y tú, señora, vencieras,
a no haber imaginado
que afrentado,
por infame aborrecieras
quien quisiste por *honrado*. (1119-36)

· · · · · · · · · · · · · · · · · · · ·

JIMENA: Sólo te culpo, agraviada,
el ver que a mis ojos vienes
a tiempo que aun fresca tienes
mi sangre en mano y espada;
   pero no a mi amor, rendido,
sino a ofenderme has llegado,
confïado
de no ser aborrecido
por lo que fuiste *adorado*. (1164-72)

The passage is too long to quote in its entirety, but a thorough study of it has convinced me that the aural guideposts so set within the text do, indeed, serve as audible signs leading the audience to understand the nature of what is happening on stage. Even those not poetically sophisticated enough to recognize the format or the reason for so using it will have had the message impressed, if only subliminally, upon their minds.

In a study of Tirso de Molina's *El condenado por desconfiado* written years ago, I noted the unusual nature of some aspects of that work's versification, particularly with regard to the use of *quintillas* in the textual presentation.[6] At that time I pointed to the

---

6. Vern G. Williamsen, "Some Odd *Quintillas* and Question of Authenticity in Tirso's Theater," *RF*, 82 (1970), 23-39.

the key structural importance of two "odd" *quintillas*. The first occurs in Act I, scene vi,[7] as the Demonio appears alone on stage to explain openly the theological basis of the conflict upon which the play is based: Paulo has a problem with his doubt and with his faith and, because, by his own free will, he has sought an answer in exact knowledge rather than in faith, he is in grave danger. The words that emphasize the nature of the problem appear in the triply repeated rhyme of the isolated *quintilla* of the fifth class (*aabba*):[8]

DEMONIO: Bien mi engaña va *trazado*.
Hoy verá el *desconfiado*
de Dios y de su poder
el fin que viene a tener,
pues él propio lo ha *buscado*.

Lope de Vega, too, seems to have used consonant rhyme words to such a purpose. In *El castigo sin venganza*, his masterfully written tragedy of 1631, for example, Lope chose *silva* of the second class to introduce the initiating incident.[9] Federico, natural son of the Duke of Ferrara, is on his way to escort his stepmother-to-be, Casandra, to Ferrara where the Duke's subjects expect that she will produce a legitimate heir to the profligate Duke. In the opening verses of the passage, the audience would certainly have heard the triple rhyming of *gusto, disgusto,* and *justo*:

BATIN: Desconozco el estilo de tu *gusto*.
¿Agora en cuatro sauces te detienes,
cuando a negocio, Federico, vienes
de tan grande importancia?
FREDERICO: Mi *disgusto*
no me permite, como fuera *justo*,
más prisa y más cuidado..... (234-239)

---

7. *Comedias de Tirso de Molina* (Madrid, 1944, *BAE V*), pp. 184-203. All textual references are to this edition. The second scene referred to in the article cited above does not seem to have been written so as to exhibit the qualities discussed here.

8. The fact that this passage is an isolated *quintilla* may be significant or it may not. It is possible that the original text had the scene set in *décima* of which we have only the final half. The rhyme words would have the same effect, however.

9. Lope de Vega, *El castigo sin venganza*, ed. C.F.A. van Dam (Salamanca, 1968). All references are to this edition.

As if this were not sufficient, the opening use of the rhyme is repeated at the end of Federico's speech when, using internal rhyme, Lope places *gusto* (on the tonically accented sixth syllable) in the same verse with *justo* and then rhymes both with *disgusto* in the following verse:

> FEDERICO: . . . . que si voy mostrando
> a nuestra gente *gusto*, como es *justo*,
> el alma llena de mortal *disgusto*,
> camino a Mantua. . . . .   (250-253)

These repeated rhymes almost surely function as a forewarning of the themes of sensual pleasure, moral distress, and implacable justice at the heart of the drama that then develops as each of the main characters struggles with the situation.[10]

In *La vida es sueño* there is evidence that Calderón, too, made good use of the audible force of rhyme words. One example in which he combines that usage with the rhetorical technique of recapitulation to good effect is found in the second act as Segismundo, in his second meeting with Rosaura—this time in her disguise as Aurora—projects his recognition of her beauty into a series of metaphors:

> SEGISMUNDO: No digas tal; di *el sol*, a cuya llama
> aquella estrella vive,
> pues de tus rayos resplandor recibe;
> yo vi en reino de olores
> que presidía entre comunes flores
> la deidad de la *rosa*,
> y era su emperatriz por más hermosa;
> yo vi entre piedras finas
> de la ·docta academia de sus minas
> preferir el *diamante*,
> y ser su emperador por más brillante;

---

10. Vern G. Williamsen, "*El castigo sin venganza* de Lope de Vega: Una tragedia novelesca," *La Chispa '83* (New Orleans, 1983), pp. 327-38.

yo en esas cortes bellas
de la inquieta república de *estrellas*,
vi en el lugar primero
por rey de las estrellas el *lucero*;
yo en esferas perfetas,
llamando el sol a cortes los *planetas*,
le vi que presidía,
como mayor oráculo del día.
¿Pues cómo si entre *flores*, entre *estrellas*,
piedras, signos, planetas, las más bellas
prefieren, tú has servido
la de menos beldad, habiendo sido
por más bella y hermosa,
sol, lucero, diamante, estrella y rosa? (1593-1617)

It should be noted that the metaphoric vehicles for each of the key elements in the system appear first in rhyme position in verses 1593-1607 with the exception of the word *sol*. *Sol* does, however, occur on the tonically accented sixth syllable of the endecasyllable. These metaphors are then reversed antonomastically in lines 1611-1612, and the entire set of vehicles is recapitulated in verse 1617. The rhetorical repetition is especially effective because the key words of the metaphorical system appear in rhyme position.[11]

11. Although I am here leaving the discussion of the relationship of rhetorical technique to strophic form to be represented by the foregoing, there are much more efficient passages that deserve to be noted and could be used as examples of the problem. The use of anaphora, for example, in the soliloquies of Segismundo in *La vida es sueño*, or its use in the passage of *El castigo sin venganza* in which Federico makes perfectly clear that he is being seduced by his stepmother and that he knows what is going on:

FEDERICO: Tú me engañas, yo me abraso;
tú me incitas, yo me pierdo;
tú me animas, yo me espanto;
tú me esfuerzas, yo me turbo;
tú me libras, yo me enlazo;
tú me llevas, yo me quedo;
tú me enseñas, yo me atajo...   (1521-27)

The effect of the anaphora is heightened by the short poetic lines in which it is set and by the doubling at the hemistich.

So far I have argued the need for recognizing the relationship between words occurring in consonantal rhyme patterns and the themes and structures of the play at hand; but assonant rhyme patterns are typical of Spanish dramatic versification as well. This is especially true of the later *comedias* since, as the seventeenth century progressed, the *redondilla* which was the work horse of the earlier plays tended to be replaced by the *romance* meter as the strophic form for the presentation of dramatic texts.[12] In fact the frequent recurrence of set vowel sounds sustained over a considerable period of time, so typical of the *romance*, may have made it a particularly useful form for imparting a specific tonal quality or coloring to the passages involved.

Damián Salucio del Poyo, in his *Privanza y caída de don Alvaro de Luna,*[13] made an interesting use of combined assonance and consonance in his presentation of King John's lament dealing with the need to sentence his friend and favorite to death. Salucio used a passage of *quintillas* of type one (*ababa*) in which the alternating lines of the entire passage were concurrently assonating in *i-e,*[14] in such a way that the passage was not only written in the *quintilla* strophe but was at the same time a *romance*. The plaintive effect of the repeated vowel sounds in rhyme position sustained throughout was certainly directed to the tonal quality so produced.

In *Los balcones de Madrid*, a play seemingly written in the 1630's that has generally been attributed to Tirso de Molina,[15] the author-poet used five passages of *romances* with a different masculine assonance (an accented final vowel rather than an accented vowel plus a final unaccented vowel). This number of

12. See the discussion of these changes in S.G. Morley and C. Bruerton, *La cronología de las comedias de Lope de Vega* (Madrid, 1968), pp. 102-25.

13. *Tercera parte de las comedias de Lope de Vega y otros autores* (Barcelona, 1612), fols. 150-66.

14. A very useful study could be made of the reasons why certain combinations of vowel sounds seem to carry with them given tonal effects. Here I remit such study to those better able to deal with the semiology involved than I.

15. *BAE*, V, pp. 556-571. All textual references are to this text, but see: Vern G. Williamsen and Harold G. Jones, "Dos refundiciones tirsianas: *Amor no teme peligros* y *Los balcones de Madrid,*" *Homenaje a Tirso* (Madrid: Revista Estudios, 1981), pp. 133-56.

masculine assonating passages in one play is odd in itself, but even stranger is that each of them features a different vowel in alphabetical order (*á, é, í, ó,* and *ú*).

The first passage occurs when Don Juan comes to complain to Doña Elisa about her apparent fickleness. The laisse begins with his threat to kill her (*matar*), goes on to her response that brings them into agreement (*conformidad*), passes on to the moment of peacemaking (*paz*), deals with their hopes for the future of their love (*vivirá*), and ends with a rather scatological joke passed between the *criada* Leonor and the *gracioso* Coral:

CORAL: ¿No habrá,
             Leonor, para mí un candil?
             Que a escuras he de maullar
             como gato entre dos puertas.
LEONOR: No hay gota en él.
CORAL: Pues serás
             virgen loca, si no hay gota,
LEONOR: ¿Y tú?
CORAL: ¿Yo? Gota coral.[16]

The second act begins with a *romance* in *é* in which the Count bribes Leonor to allow him into Elisa's apartment. The third passage in *í* (Act II, *iii*) comes about a short time later when with Don Juan hidden in her closet and the Count in her alcove, Elisa's father enters the *aposento* with the third suitor for her hand, Don Pedro. Leonor tricks Elisa into claiming a previous agreement to marry the Count. Key rhyme words in this passage, a tissue of lies and double-dealing, are *encubrir, corregir, arrepentir, ardid, fingir,* and *sutil*. The act ends (scene *x*) with a passage of *romances* in *ó*, in which Coral reports to Don Juan the scene of recriminations between Elisa and her father and the father's later plotting to get the Count to marry her after all. Coral then passes on to his plans for ensuring the success of Don Juan's suit providing that he still does want her for himself. Coral will buld a drawbridge with which to connect the two balconies and allow the

16. P. 561a.

lovers access to each other's rooms in the adjoining houses. Key rhymes are noted in such words as *amor, posesión, balcón, arquitector, ensamblador* and *invención.*

The third act has the very unusual passage of *romances* in *ú* (scene *iv*)[17] in an essentially comic scene, one in which Coral urges Don Juan to action in the matter at hand:

> CORAL: Encajado el pasadizo
> que ha de ser nuestro arcaduz,
> y de balcón a balcón
> echó mi solicitud;
> por más que encarcele el viejo
> a tu Elisa, si tahur
> eres, a figura estás
> yendo a primera de flux.

Even more certainly than as a tonal device the *romance* came into use as an audible signal of the impending close of a *comedia* written in the heydey of the genre (1600-1650). According to Morley and Bruerton, Lope typically used romances to end each act of a play, especially those written after 1609. Lope's use of the meter to close each act of a *comedia* can be summarized as follows:[18]

Plays written before 1598	5.7%
Plays written 1599-1603	19.1%
Plays written before 1604	11.7%
Plays written 1604-1608	36.7%
Plays written 1609-1618	82.7%
Plays written 1620-1625	92.5%
Plays written 1626-1635	96.7%

Unfortunately, Morley and Bruerton left no data dealing specifically with the endings of the plays as distinguished from

17. This assonance from (*ú*) does not appear in any of the plays written by Lope de Vega or attributed to him. See Morley and Bruerton, p. 125.
18. Morley and Bruerton, pp. 201-206.

those of the act endings; however, figures that I have gathered from Tirso de Molina's theater may well be taken as representative of the period 1600-1635 since all of his plays were all but certainly written within that time span. Of the eighty-seven *comedias* and *auto sacramentales* attributed to Tirso (we have fewer texts than that to be taken as authentically Tirso's since we know some of these to be erroneously attributed to him), only eight do not end in romances. Two of these are early works, two are late pieces, and four are of dubious attribution. These figures show that there was general agreement between Lopean and Tirsian practices and they do deal specifically with the ending laisses of the plays.

Interesting, also, is the fact that, in Tirso's works at least, only a few of the many possible assonant rhyme schemes seem to predominate in these final passages. The assonances most commonly appearing in them are those in *a-a* (20 cases), *e-a* (thirteen cases) or in forms assonating with the final words or a key word in the title (37 cases).[19] This leads one to suspect that, once the audiences became accustomed to the procedure, whenever they heard a romance of this typically closing type, well into the third act, they would expect a prompt conclusion of the play. The poets could then react to those expectations in such a way as to prolong suspense or to bring about an unexpected close to the play by varying the pattern. Indeed this may well explain such instances as Tirso's *La venganza de Tamar* in which, well into the third act, there is a passage of romances in *á* rhyming with the title word. This would normally have indicated the approaching end, but Tirso moves from this strophic form to a passage of *redondillas* and one of *décimas* before returning to the final laisse of romance in *e-o*. This technique seems to approach what, in music, would be referred to as a false cadence: a signal of the approaching close (in music repeated reference to the dominant chord that requires

19. These data might be even more highly indicative of a relationship between the title of a *comedia* and the closing assonance if we took into account the fact that many of the plays are not now known by the same title they carried in the Golden Age. For example, see the article referred to in note 15 above. Tirso's *La firmeza en la hermosura* was certainly played most frequently under the title *Amor no teme peligros*. The title of *La firmeza* seems to have become attached to the work sometime late in the seventeenth, during the eighteenth, or even as late as the nineteenth century.

resolution to the tonic) is sidetracked for the presentation of new information before arriving at the true ending. Tirso uses this same method in at least four other plays written after 1621: *Antona García, Por el sótano y el torno, La celosa de sí misma*, and *Siempre ayuda la verdad*. Tirso was not alone in using the process, as is witnessed by the "false cadences" in Calderón's plays *El médico de su honra* and *La vida es sueño* as well as in those of many other dramatists of the time.

Sometimes rather than being the rhyme words or assonating vowel sounds that merit discussion in any treatment of the versification of a given *comedia*, the rhythmic effects achieved by the poet may be the poetic element most worthy of comment. For instance the mocking verses in *arte mayor* of Mira de Amescua's *Primera parte de don Alvaro de Luna*[20] in which the gracioso Pablillos comments on the opening dedicatory verses ("Al muy prepotente don Juan el segundo") of Juan de Mena's *Trescientas* as read by Mena at the court of Juan II:

PABLILLOS: ¡Ay!, que me mata aquel *prepotente*,
               pudiendo decir: *al muy poderoso*:
               ¡Ay, ay!, que ese metro es tono famoso
               para los ciegos cantar de repente, [sic][21]
               ¡Ay, ay!, que ya temo que pueda la gente
               oír tales versos sin dar aullidos,
               tirando los bancos por mal admitidos.
MENA: Atiende, y no hables, bufón imprudente.
               (II, 381-88)

The parodic value of the rhythms employed here was certainly intended to increase their humorous effect.

In Mira's very early play, *La rueda de la Fortuna*, he employed unusual blank verse in *esdrújulos* for the speech in which the general Leoncio harangues his troops, whipping them up into the spirit of battle. They conclude:

LEONCIO: Eximid, eximid nuestra república
               del tirano poder de aqueste sátrapa,

---

20. Ed. Nellie Sánchez Arce (Mexico, 1964).
21. The verse is hypometrical. It should probably be read as *para los ciegos que cantan de repente.*

> que a Roma desampara y al Pontífice.
> ¡Viva la gloria del eterno Artífice![22]

Mira later used this same odd form of verse to good effect for presenting the analogous scene in which Goliath makes his grotesque challenge to the Hebrew troops in *El arpa de David*.[23]

I hope that I have indicated here some additional channels through which to explore those areas commented upon so intelligently by Victor Dixon in his paper. Dixon quite correctly calls for introductions to scholarly editions that do more than present the raw data of a play's versification. He asks that discussion be directed to the esthetic purpose and the poetic effects achieved by the poet-dramatist. Essentially, he has asked that we study the relationship of verse form to theme, mood, tonal quality, intensity of action, decorum, and the structural features of the plays. In the preceding, I hope that I have expanded upon that call to reason and have exemplified some of the directions such discussions might reasonably take. It will only be after many more editions with carefully wrought introductory studies have been prepared that we will be able to approach with sensitivity and security a comprehension of the marvelous polymetric language of the *comedia*.

Dixon has, moreover, indicated that versification data can serve for more than esthetic discussion, that it can become one more link in a chain of positivistic evidence supporting or denying an attribution of authorship or indicating a proposed date of composition for the play being discussed. He has quite correctly made a case for the need to study thoroughly the versification habits of a given author as exhibited in his known works if we are to make use of such positivistic data. I would like to add a plea for even greater care and two cautionary notes. Dixon has properly footnoted the major sources for gaining an introductory overview of the problem and the bibliography on the subject of Spanish versification, including studies of internal line structures (his notes 39 and 42). I would only add to his listing that one should certainly

---

22. *BAE*, 45, p. 15bc.
23. Mira de Amescua, *El arpa de David*, ed. C.E. Anibal (Columbus, Ohio, 1925), pp. 41-42.

refer to the on-going work of John B. Woolridge and to the series of doctoral studies done in recent years under the direction of Donald McGrady at the University of Virginia as examples of the kinds of evidentiary studies that can and should be done.[24]

One should, however, keep in mind that although habits of versification did vary markedly among various dramatists (Ruiz de Alarcón certainly used much higher percentages of *redondillas* than did any of his contemporaries), that the range in usage for each of the major strophic forms for any one poet is bound to overlap the usage figures for many others (Alarcón used a range of 20-90% *redondillas* with an average near 60%; Mira de Amescua used a range of 3-78% *redondillas* with an average of near 40%). This is especially true when a poet's career spanned a longer time period, as is the case for Lope de Vega, Mira de Amescua, and Guillén de Castro.[25]

If one were to use the patterns of change discerned by Morley and Bruerton for Lope's usage throughout his career as a basic chronological gauge typical for any play written between 1588 and 1635, he might not be far wrong in general. The dramatists certainly followed the leader in matters versificatory. As Lope's use of *redondillas* dropped and his use of *romances* increased, so did that of others. When Lope cut his use of blank verse to very low levels, the form all but disappeared from the works of his contemporaries. In other words, although there are definite differences between poets in their use of strophic forms, there are concurrent changes in style and mode reflected within the works of all poets. This problem of compounded variables is a very difficult one to deal with and is made even more complex by at least two additional facts: (1) any poet, for some reason or whim, might choose to do something different from what he had always done, or (2) an artistic writer might well react against the constraints placed upon him by any codified system. For example, the *silva* seems to have been accepted as a useful form for dramatic purposes only some time in the decade of the 1620's.

24. See for example the published dissertation of Augusto A. Portuondo, *Diez comedias atribuidas a Lope de Vega: Estudio de su autenticidad* (Charlottesville, VA, 1980).

25. These data are taken from my studies of the versification of Alarcón, Mira de Amescua, Guillén de Castro and others, not as yet published.

Lope himself made no considerable use of the form except for an occasional laisse in *silva* of the third class (a form more closely related to blank verse than to the *silva* itself) until the very end of his writing career (1629-35).[26] However, Mira de Amescua in *La casa del tahur*, a play written shortly after his return from Italy in 1616, used slightly more than fourteen per cent *silva* II. This is the heaviest use of the *silva* for any play written before 1625 of which I am aware. The critical questions that logically evolve from such an unusual procedure are: Was Mira's long absence from the Madrid scene or his experience in Italy responsible for the abrupt change? Was the change he thus introduced accepted by the public? Did he influence others who followed to adopt the new form? Because we lack sufficient data, it is difficult even to hazard a guess at the answers.

The consequence of all this is that we must be extremely careful in using the positivistic evidence provided by the versification of a given work in making any firm conclusions. It is only because of the vast field of texts they had in which to mine data that Morley and Bruerton were able to set a Lopean chronology that has yet to be challenged in any major way. Yet, even with the mountain of facts they had at hand, they were very careful about accepting any attribution of a work to Lope on the positive hypothesis. Much more certain as a procedure is the proof of the negative. We cannot say now, and perhaps we never will be able to do so, that a given text was written by a certain poet on evidence provided by its versification. We can say, however, that there is logical basis to be found in the data for concluding that a given poet probably did not write the text at hand. In this case, the more different a text at hand is from a poet's usual habits of versification as judged from the works we know to be his, the more certain we can be that he did not write it. Because of the massive evidence they had at hand, Morley and Bruerton, for example, reject any play attributed to Lope if it contains a passage of *silva* of the first type (regularly alternating seven and eleven syllable verses rhymed in couplets).[27] Similarly, but more carefully, because of the

26. Morley and Bruerton, pp. 139-42, 173.
27. Morley and Bruerton, p. 139.

much more limited canon of Tirsian works, I concluded years ago that the versification of *El condenado por desconfiado* was sufficiently different from Tirso's habitual practices that we should see the data as one element on the side of those denying the attribution of the play to him, but that it was not so different that the variances could not be explained by the editorial history of the text; therefore, the attribution could not be denied to Tirso only on the basis of the verse forms employed in its composition.[28]

The final set of points made by Dixon deal with the editor's knowledge of Spanish versification as an aid to the establishment of text. Such knowledge is, indeed, basic to any editor's work as he approaches such textual problems as variants, missing lines, etc. The editor must be aware not only of the general principles of Spanish metrics as described by many who have worked with the *comedia*, but also with the fine points of variable rhyme forms that were permissible at the time the work was written and the many possible rhythmic arrangements of the Spanish line. There is ample evidence to be found in some recent editions that the editors involved did not have the requisite knowledge and, therefore, have been responsible for the insertion of errors into the text, wrong interpretations of the text, or for perpetuating errors found in earlier editions.[29] A good editor will also be thoroughly familiar with the individual peculiarities of the versification of the poet whose work he is dealing with.

In a recent edition of Calderón's *El príncipe constante*, reference to the table of verse forms that is found in the introduction prepared by the editor would lead one to believe that Calderón had included six passages of *quintillas* in the play much against his usual practice of using that strophic form quite sparsely. Such is not the case. The first three passages that are so identified are sets of *décimas*, a form Calderón employed much

---

28. See note 6 above.

29. In the passage that follows I cite the following editions. Because I wish to focus on the kinds of problems involved rather than to point a finger at the editors involved, I omit reference to them by name. Calderón de la Barca, *El príncipe constante*, Madrid: Espasa Calpe (Clásicos Castellanos, 204), 1975; Mira de Amescua, *La fe de Hungría* and *El monte de la piedad*, New Orleans: Tulane University (Tulane Studies in Romance Languages and Literature. 7), 1975: Calderón de la Barca, *La hija del aire*, London: Támesis (Colección Támesis: Serie B-Textos, 9), 1970.

more frequently. I suspect that at one time in the editing process, the editor was fully aware of the case since the *décimas* are set off into groups of ten verses (as Dixon recommends). Almost certainly, recognizing the true strophic designation for the passage would have resulted in some changes in punctuation (and the textual interpretation that implies) since in a normal *décima* there is an all but obligatory stop after the fourth verse. When this stop does not occur, that fact, too, merits discussion. In *El príncipe constante* there are two passages of *quintillas* early in the third act,[30] but the sixth passage so identified in the introduction and in the notes to the text is again a passage of *décimas*, this time garbled *décimas*, in which a correct identification of the strophe would have pointed to rather extensive cuts in the base text from which the edited text derives. In this case the matter becomes more important because there are available other early and reliable texts in which the passage is not so badly mangled. A recognition of the true strophic form would have aided in the re-establishment of a finer text.

In a recent edition of Mira de Amescua's *La fe de Hungría*, the result of erroneous interpretation of verse form is a faulty table of versification. The editor has included, for example, a song of irregular form as if it were made up of its constituent parts. He lists ten "versos pareados rimados en versos fluctuantes," one "verso en latín" (it is Greek!), six more "versos pareados..." and a final *redondilla* (vv. 332-352). The passage is a song with repeated refrain, and the final lines are not at all a *redondilla*. The table is further complicated because the editor lists a seventeen-verse *soneto con estrambote* as a *soneto*, one *verso suelto*, and a *pareado*. Yet he has failed to comment on what is the most unusual aspect of the passage: the sonnet breaks the basic rule of Italianate Spanish verse in that every line ends with an accented syllable rather than the required feminine ending. The irregularity is not in the basic form but in the structure of the individual lines!

One further example of the kinds of problems we, as editors and as scholars attempting to use the work of other editors, must

---

30. In view of Diego Marín's findings with regard to Calderón's versification (see note 2 above), these two passages of *quintillas* merit study to see if they do, indeed, function as Marín has reported in the case of other plays.

guard against will suffice. In an edition of Calderón's *La hija del aire*, in many places (in more than 200 locations within the text) the editor has accepted erroneous readings from earlier texts or inserted his own. Examples abound, such as the dieresis indicated in verse 2369 of Part I that makes the octosyllable into a hypermetrical line. The dieresis goes completely against Calderón's usual practice in the use of internal line structures. What is needed instead is a syneresis in the word *apear* (making it a bisyllable rather than the usual trisyllable, a practice that is Calderonian) in order to shorten the line as it stands:

> ARSIDAS: Ya la música otra vez
> suena, ya se apean.
> NINO: Dichoso (2380)
> . . . .

Also in Part I the use of a dieresis in verse 2466 ("muy tarde hoy le oïgo) is hardly correct since the word is in rhyme position in a laisse of *romance* in *o-o*. Also in a passage of romance (*e-o*) in Part II, the editor, citing no source for such a change, destroys the assonance completely because he prefers a different subject for the verb:

> LIDORO: No *puedo*
> excusar aquí el seguir
> —Perdóname si te *ofendo*— (not *ofende*)
> la voz común. . . . . (210-13)

This editor, too, makes the mistake of classifying *décimas* as *quintillas* (Part II, 2905-84) with the same results as mentioned above. The result of such inattention to matters of versification is a text that is all but unusable since it is even more unreliable than the earlier texts upon which it is based.

Editing the text of a Spanish Golden Age *comedia*, whether based on an autograph, on contemporary playscripts, or on variously edited and printed texts, is an arduous task. By no means the least onerous is the preparation necessary in order to treat the play's versification with the scholarship and the respect it deserves not only as an artifice but as a tool. As an aid to the editor, a knowledge of the mechanical techniques of Spanish verse as well as of the compositional habits of the poet concerned can serve as a means of establishing the correct text. A knowledge of the poet's particular habits as well as of the historical development of the polymetric system employed in the Spanish *comedia* can help in establishing a date of composition or to reject an erroneous attribution. These literary historical and textual matters are, after all, the basis upon which literary criticism depends as it moves into more interesting philosophical and esthetic fields of effort. Such mechanistic knowledge is absolutely necessary to the editor as he prepares his introductory materials and turns to addressing the artistic purposes that were served by the multi-strophic textual presentation: (1) as audible signals of structural divisions within the work, (2) as a means of achieving needed tonal effects and variety, (3) as the vehicles through which the rhetoric employed took shape, and (4) as the means by which, through rhythm and rhyme, certain words and ideas were made to strike the public ear. It does not matter whether the audience then, or we now, are completely aware of the artifice being employed. Now, just as then, some who came into contact with the text are fully alert to what is going on, others are completely oblivious to the technical aspects of textual presentation. It doesn't even matter whether or not the poet consciously knew the reasons behind his choices of strophic forms, rhymes, or rhythms. I believe that I have shown here that the effects achieved, even on a subliminal level, were and are truly effective and dramatically efficient. This is the marvel of the multi-strophic texts of the Spanish *comedia*!

STAGING AND STAGE DIRECTIONS

J. E. Varey

Despite the assiduous labours of nineteenth- and twentieth-century scholars, the study of the drama of Spain's Golden Age is still beset with numerous problems. One of the major problems is that of chronology, another is bibliographical, and a third area in which much remains to be done is the study of the staging conditions of the period. In this article I shall examine the problems of editing a seventeeth-century play from the point of view of staging, concentrating on the *mise-en-scène* of the commercial theatres, the *corrales de comedias*, and the Court theatre.

Various sources of information are available. A large corpus of documents—far greater than that available to the student of the Elizabethan and Jacobean stage—has been preserved in archives and libraries. Much has been published or extracted over the years by various hands, but important archives are virtually unexplored. In the nineteenth century, Cotarelo y

Mori and Pérez Pastor published a great quantity of documentation, but, in accordance with the style of their age, did so selectively. More recently, N.D. Shergold and I have set about the task of publishing full catalogues of the material available in Madrid, in the series entitled *Fuentes para la historia del teatro en España*[1]. Whilst inevitably much of the documentation is concerned with finance, the papers which appear in that series do have a considerable bearing on the staging of plays. Of direct importance for a knowledge of staging conditions are the two important articles by Shergold which publish the documents relating to the repairs of the two Madrid theatres, the Corral de la Cruz and the Corral del Príncipe[2]. The two theatres date from 1579 and 1583 respectively. However, the Ayuntamiento did not take over responsibility for them from the Hospitals until 1638, and it is for this reason that the repair documents are not preserved prior to 1641. We thus lack direct evidence of this kind for the earlier period. The original *Libro del gasto del teatro que se hace nuevo para las comedias en la calle del Príncipe*, which survived in the archive of the Hospitals and passed with other documentation to the Archivo de la Diputación Provincial, was destroyed in the Civil War[3]. Two plans have been preserved, one of each of the two theatres, dating from 1735[4]. The investigator is thus faced with the

1. N.D. Shergold and J.E. Varey, *Fuentes para la historia del teatro en España. I. Representaciones palaciegas: 1603-1699. Estudio y documentos* (London, 1982); J.E.V. and N.D.S., *Fuentes para la historia del teatro en España. III. Teatros y comedias en Madrid: 1600-1650. Estudio y documentos* (London, 1971); J.E.V. and N.D.S., *Fuentes para la historia del teatro en España. IV. Teatros y comedias en Madrid: 1651-1655. Estudio y documentos* (London, 1973); J.E.V. and N.D.S., *Fuentes para la historia del teatro en España. V. Teatros y comedias en Madrid: 1666-1687. Estudio y documentos* (London, 1974); N.D.S. and J.E.V., *Fuentes para la historia del teatro en España. VI. Teatros y comedias en Madrid: 1687-1699. Estudio y documentos* (London, 1979); J.E.V., *Fuentes para la historia del teatro en España. VII. Los títeres y otras diversiones populares de Madrid: 1758-1840. Estudio y documentos* (London, 1972).

2. N.D. Shergold, "Nuevos documentos sobre los corrales de comedias de Madrid en el siglo XVII", *RBAM*, 20 (1951), 391-445; N.D.S., "Nuevos documentos sobre los corrales de comedias de Madrid, 1652-1700", *Boletín de la Biblioteca de Menéndez Pelayo*, 35 (1959), 209-346.

3. Casiano Pellicer, *Tratado histórico sobre el origen y progresos de la comedia y del histrionismo en España* (Madrid, 1804), vol. I, p. 66.

4. First published by J.E. Varey and N.D. Shergold, "Tres dibujos inéditos de los antiguos corrales de comedias de Madrid", *RBAM*, 20 (1951), 319-20.

problem of working backwards from the two architectural drawings, using the evidence from the repairs and other documents, in an attempt to elucidate the staging conditions of earlier years. Recently John J. Allen has produced a study of the Corral del Príncipe, a major attempt to reconstruct the theatre based on this evidence.[5]

A second source is that of eye-witnesses. Various travellers who visited Madrid during the course of the seventeenth century deal cursorily with the popular theatres; the accounts of the visits of Brunel (1655), Bertaut (1659) and the chronicler of Cosme de Médicis (1668-69) are the most important[6]. Mme. d'Aulnoy's account of Spain, although much quoted, was discredited by Fouché-Delbosc[7]. No contemporary illustration, such as the De Witt drawing of the English stage, survives.

A third source is that of the stage directions of the plays themselves. But stage directions give rise to a series of difficulties. The date of composition of most plays is uncertain, and it is only rarely that we can say that a particular play was written for performance in a specific theatre in a definite year. Here the question of the transmission of texts—dealt with below—is relevant. The investigator can only speak in general terms, stating, for example, that the text of many plays requires the use of a balcony (*lo alto del teatro*). What we cannot say is whether a balcony existed in the same state over a definite number of years, nor is there documentary evidence of its first construction, redesigning or rebuilding. The Madrid repair documents indicate that the structures of the theatres were under constant repair, and the clauses in the lease documents indicate the ways in which *autores de comedias* adapted the stage to meet the requirements of

5. John J. Allen, *El Corral del Príncipe (1583-1744). The Reconstruction of a Spanish Golden Age Playhouse* (Gainesville, Florida, 1983).

6. A. de Brunel, *Voyage d'Espagne, curieux, historique, et politique. Fait en l'année 1655* (Paris, 1665); François Bertaut, *Relation d'un voyage d'Espagne ou est exactement décrit l'Estat de la Cour de ce Royaume, et de son gouvernement* (Paris, 1664); François Bertaut, *Journal du voyage d'Espagne* (Paris, 1669); and Angel Sánchez Rivero and Angela Mariutti de Sánchez Rivero (eds), *Viaje de Cosme de Médicis por España y Portugal 1668-1669* (Madrid, 1933).

7. Madame d'Aulnoy, *Relation du voyage d'Espagne*, ed. R. Foulché-Delbosc (Paris, 1926).

the plays they wished to produce[8]. The two theatres should not therefore be considered as static structures. Nevertheless, the text of a play and its stage directions can point to general staging conditions, particularly if several plays produce similar evidence. Provided that we bear continually in mind the problems of chronology and the lack of hard factual evidence concerning major portions of the stage, we can, with due circumspection, use the evidence of text and stage directions to flesh out the documentary sources.

I have so far concentrated on Madrid. Valuable studies have been published on the theatre in Seville, Valencia, Valladolid and other major cities. Shergold's important study, *A History of the Spanish Stage from Medieval Times until the End of the Seventeenth Century* (Oxford: Clarendon, 1967) represents a major step forward in our understanding of the staging of plays in the commercial theatres. Since the publication of that volume, investigations have continued or are in hand in other archives, and all will broaden our understanding of the problems involved.

Finally, the student of the Spanish stage has the advantage— enjoyed nowhere else in Europe—of being able to visit in Almagro a *corral de comedias* re-discovered in the early 1950s and, apparently, only lightly restored. By visiting this theatre, problems of sight-lines, acoustics and spatial relationships can be more easily understood. What is now needed is a detailed architectural study of that theatre, with full plans and illustrations, together with a detailed account of the works undertaken between its re-discovery and its opening to the public.

Drawing together all this evidence, it is possible to visualise in the commercial theatres of the seventeenth century a platform stage, projecting into the audience which surrounded it on three sides. Across the back of the stage ran a balcony, supported by

8. J.E. Varey and N.D. Shergold, "Datos históricos sobre los primeros teatros de Madrid: contratos de arriendo, 1587-1615", *BH*, 60 (1958), 73-95; J.E.V. and N.D.S., "Datos históricos sobre los primeros teatros de Madrid: contratos de arriendo, 1615-1641", *BH*, 62 (1960), 168-89; J.E.V. and N.D.S., "Datos históricos sobre los primeros teatros de Madrid: prohibiciones de autos y comedias y sus consecuencias (1664-1651)", *BH*, 72 (1960), 286-325; J.E.V. and N.D.S., "Datos históricos de los primeros teatros de Madrid: contratos de arriendo, 1641-1719", *Boletín de la Biblioteca de Menéndez Pelayo*, 39 (1963), 95-179.

pillars, with a second balcony above the first. The space below the lower balcony was curtained off. Through these curtains actors entered the stage through two "doors" at the left and right rear of the stage (although we should, in spite of many stage directions which speak of *puertas*, visualise gaps in the curtains rather than wooden doors set in their frames). Between these two entrances, the curtains could be drawn back to reveal a discovery-space, used to exhibit scenes of violence, allegorical settings, elaborate stage machines, or to permit the bringing out on to the platform stage of bulky properties. The discovery space could equally serve as a cave or prison[9]. Trapdoors were located in the platform stage and in the discovery space. Many plays postulate a means of access from the platform stage to the balcony in the sight of the audience (a problem which is not yet totally resolved); others indicate that the actors had access to the balcony from behind the stage. The second balcony could be used for cloud machines, controlled by ropes which ran over pulleys, the counterweights hidden behind the pillars which supported the stage. Many plays use no "scenery" in the modern sense, but stage directions in other plays indicate a more "realistic" approach, with the use of greenery, imitation mountains, and so forth. But the majority of those plays which are nowadays recognised as the great achievements of the Spanish theatre use the bare stage, "painting" the setting through the verses and images of the text of the plays.

* * *

The evidence available for the study of the Court theatre in Spain in the seventeenth century is scant, in comparison with that which is available for the student of the Court theatres of Italy, France and England. In the early years of the seventeenth century great Court entertainments were given on specially constructed stages in the royal palaces. Villamediana's *La gloria de Niquea* and Hurtado de Mendoza's *Querer por sólo querer*, performed in Aranjuez in 1622, were put on on stages built for the one

---

9. J.E. Varey, "Cavemen in Calderón (and some cavewomen)", in *Approaches to the Theater of Calderón*, ed. Michael D. McGaha (Washington, D.C., 1982), 231-47.

performance[10]. The stages for these and similar plays were intended to serve for the unique occasion. Plays were performed in the gardens of the Buen Retiro in the 1630s, again using stages designed for a single performance[11]. Other Court entertainments combined elements of the play and the masque, such as Bocángel's *La piedra cándida*, put on in Madrid in 1647[12]. But from the early years of the seventeenth century the Court was also entertained by professional actors who staged in the Royal apartments plays currently in repertoire in the commercial theatres[13]. A recent article by José Simón Díaz has brought to light an account of one of these performances, which clearly indicates that the staging conditions, given the limitations of a performance in the royal apartments, were not very different from those in the contemporary *corrales de comedias*[14].

But in 1636-1640 the great hall of the old Alcázar was refurbished, and became known thereafter as the Salón dorado[15]: a dismountable theatre was built for performances therein and, taking its name from the Salón, became known as the Teatro dorado[16]. During these same years, the Coliseo of the Buen Retiro was constructed, and opened its doors in 1640[17].

The two theatres of the Salón dorado and the Coliseo had much in common: both were designed with a very definite proscenium arch, both used visible-change stage machinery, with flats, shutters and drop scenes, and both were capable of astonishing stage effects. Núñez de Castro writes: "En las Comedias de tramoyas, que han admirado la Corte, el objeto mas delicioso a la vista, han sido las mudanças totales del Teatro, ya

10. Shergold, *History*, pp. 268-72.
11. Shergold, *History*, pp. 278-86.
12. Shergold, *History*, pp. 302-03.
13. N.D. Shergold and J.E. Varey, *Fuentes I*, doc. núm. 10, pp. 47-48 and 233-35; N.D.S. and J.E.V., "Some Palace Performances of Seventeenth-Century Plays", *BHS*, 40 (1963), 212-44.
14. José Simón Díaz, "Autos sacramentales y comedias palaciegas y de Colegio en el Madrid de 1626 según un copero pontificio", *Segismundo*, 27-32 (1978-80), 85-102.
15. Juan Vélez de Guevara, *Los celos hacen estrellas*, ed. J.E. Varey and N.D. Shergold, with an ed. of the music by Jack Sage (London, 1970), lx-lxii.
16. Vélez de Guevara, *Los celos*, lxxxv-lxxxviii, and plate 1.
17. Jonathan Brown and J. H. Elliott, *A Palace for a King. The Buen Retiro and the Court of Philip IV* (New Haven, 1980).

proponiendo vn Palacio a los ojos, ya vn Iardin, ya vn Bosque, ya vn Rio picando con arrebatado curso sus corrientes, ya vn Mar inquieto en borrascas, ya sossegado en suspensa calma"[18]. Nevertheless, there was one great difference between them. The machinery of the Coliseo was the more elaborate, with winches and capstans below stage controlling the wings, and cranes and cloud-machines above the flats which permitted the achievement of aerial effects. Such machinery could not be used in the Salón dorado, for the theatre was raised only slightly above the floor of the room, and below the Salón were the *covachuelas*, or offices of the royal administration. The cut-out design of the proscenium of this theatre, clearly visible in an illustration by Herrera the Younger, did not permit the use of cloud machines, the machinery for which would have been visible above the proscenium.

Until very recently, only one set of illustrations of the Spanish Court theatre was known, that for a late (1690) performance in Valencia of a Calderón play, *La fiera, el rayo y la piedra*[19]. But now five water-colours of a performance of Juan Vélez de Guevara's *Los celos hacen estrellas*, performed in the Salón dorado in 1672, have been published[20], and in 1977 Phyllis Dearborn Massar brought to light a series of designs by Baccio del Bianco for the performance in the Coliseo of the Buen Retiro of Calderón's *Andrómeda y Perseo*[21]. We can therefore visualise much more clearly than heretofore the visual impact of these Court spectacles, and, with the aid of these illustrations, flesh out the texts of other similar Court spectacular plays.

* * *

Before looking at the way in which a modern editor should approach the problems presented by stage directions, it is

18. Alonso Núñez de Castro, *Libro historico politico. Solo Madrid es Corte, y el Cortesano en Madrid*, 2nd. ed. (Madrid, 1669), 14-15.

19. Angel Valbuena Prat, "La escenografía de una comedia de Calderón", *Archivo Español de Arte*, 16 (1930), 1-16.

20. See note 15, above.

21. Phyllis Dearborn Massar, "Scenes for a Calderón Play by Baccio del Bianco", *Master Drawings*, 15, no. 4 (1977), 365-75 and Plates 21-31.

necessary to consider the way in which texts were transmitted. A dramatist wrote a play, usually at the behest of an *autor de comedias*, and, in so doing, would in all probability have in mind the particular acting resources of a company[22] and the staging conditions of the theatre in which the play was to be presented. Undoubtedly he would construct his play in a very different way if he were writing for a Court theatre, as opposed to a *corral*. Once he had handed over the script to the actors, he had no further control over it. At some later date, probably when the *autor* felt that the commercial possibilities of the play were near exhaustion, or perhaps when temporarily short of funds, the *autor* would sell plays to a printer, who would then prepare a volume for the press, either of the plays of an individual author, or of a number of authors (the series of *Comedias diferentes* and *Comedias escogidas*). But in between these two events—the writing of the play and its printing—a number of changes could be introduced into the text.

Plays intended for one set of acting conditions might be put on elsewhere, and thus require reshaping: a good example is Calderón's *El mágico prodigioso*, originally intended for staging on carts as part of a festivity, but printed in a form which suggests that the text available to the printers had been adapted for use in the *corrales de comedias*. The first stage direction of the autograph manuscript, written for performance in the town of Yepes in 1637 to celebrate the feast of Corpus Christi, reads: "Suena un clarín a una parte de la plaza, y entra por ella un carro pintado de llamas de fuego, tirado de dos dragones, y en él sentado el Demonio. Empieza a representar desde el carro y salta en el tablado, como lo dicen los versos." The whole of this first episode (pp. 213-14, note 1)[23] is omitted from the printed text (*Escogidas XX*, 1663). Towards the end of Act I, Florio and Lelio come on stage, *de noche, cada uno por su puerta*; each separately identifies a noise as coming from a "ventana" or "balcón", the Devil appears *al balcón, baja por una escalera* and *se hunde*, i.e., disappears through a trap-door

---

22. N.D. Shergold, "*La vida es sueño*: ses acteurs, son théâtre et son public", in *Dramaturgie et Société*, ed. Jean Jacquot (Paris, 1968), I, 93-109.

23. Quotations are from Pedro Calderón de la Barca, *Comedias religiosas, I. La devoción de la Cruz y El mágico prodigioso*, ed. Angel Valbuena, Clásicos Castellanos 106 (Madrid, 1931).

(lines 886-927). This is typical *corral* staging, and would be difficult to perform on carts. The text has clearly been rewritten to accomodate the staging needs of the commercial theatre. A palace play might be revived with new scenery, with or without the active cooperation of the authors. N.D. Shergold has studied Calderón's *Siquis y Cupido* and shown how the author added new material for a performance in 1679; he has argued that the printed text in the Vera Tassis edition derives from this later performance, and is not that of the *estreno*[24]. These two examples are indicative of the way in which the repetition of a play at a later date in different stage conditions can affect the text of the play, and thus how the printed text is not always a reliable guide to the first intentions of the author.

But plays were also changed for other reasons. Some changes are the result of censorship[25]; others reflect the requirements of the company. Speeches might be cut as too long, or developed; new speeches might be added to suit the particular actors available. J.M. Ruano de la Haza has recently shown that Escamilla, the comic actor, wrote in a larger part for the *gracioso* into Act III of Calderón's *Cada uno para sí* in a surviving manuscript[26]. And the copying of the original text by the *apuntador*, who in most companies appears to have been charged with making copies and preparing the scripts from which the actors learned their roles (*sacar la comedia por papeles*), might well introduce errors by careless copying, or deliberately add or subtract material. It is not difficult to imagine how, over a relatively short period, a text could thus evolve well away from the original intentions of the author.

The scripts which were handed to a printer could thus be adulterated, and not represent the original intentions of the dramatist. Lope de Vega, as is well known, complained about the quality of the texts of the plays which came out in the early *Partes* of his plays[27]. Calderón, similarly, showed concern for the way in which

24. N.D. Shergold, "Calderón and Vera Tassis", *HR*, 22 (1955), 212-18.

25. E.M. Wilson, "Calderón and the Stage-Censor in the Seventeenth Century. A provisional study", *Symposium*, 15 (1961), 165-84.

26. Pedro Calderón de la Barca, *Cada uno para sí*, ed. José M. Ruano de la Haza, Teatro del Siglo de Oro. Ediciones críticas, 1 (Kassel, 1982), 59-60.

27. In the Prologue to *Parte XV* of his plays (Madrid, 1621), Lope refers to works of his published without authorisation as "flores del campo de su Vega que sin cultura nacen"; Hugo A. Rennert and Américo Castro, *Vida de Lope de Vega (1562-1635)* (Madrid, 1919), 283.

the early *Partes* of his plays were edited[28]. Lope also refers to the existence of the *memorión*, who would pirate a play by committing it to memory as he heard it performed. A text of *Peribáñez* which appears to be the result of an attempt to reconstruct a play from memory has recently been studied by Ruano[29]. Leaving aside such large-scale attempts to reconstruct an entire play, it is quite possible that a part of a play might be lost, and the actors forced to reconstruct the lines on the missing pages. Ruano's study of Act III of *Cada uno para sí* has demonstrated that the version published in 1661 in *Escogidas XV* is evidently shorter than Calderón had originally intended, and that this might have been due to the loss of part of the manuscript in use by the actors.

When the printer came to set up the play, he often tried to compress the text, especially if it was to appear as a *suelta*[30]. Stage directions are particularly at risk, as forming part of a play which can be compressed, or omitted altogether, notably where long lines of poetry are to be set, and this may account to some extent for the paucity of stage directions in many printed texts. It must also be remembered that many autograph manuscripts are short on stage directions, no doubt because the dramatist knew full well how the play would be staged, and the *autor de comedias* did not feel the need for precise instructions such as those which appear in many late nineteenth-century or twentieth-century plays (for example, the long and detailed stage directions of George Bernard Shaw).

A comparison of, for instance, the text of *Las fortunas de Andrómeda y Perseo*, printed by Vera Tassis in *Parte VI* (1683) of Calderón's works after his death, with the manuscript of *Andrómeda y Perseo* in the Houghton Library shows clearly that, in

28. Prologue to the *Cuarta parte* of his plays (Madrid, 1672): "No solo hallè en sus impressiones, q[ue] ya no eran mias las que lo fueron; pero muchas que no lo fueron, impressas como mias, no contentandose los hurtos de la prensa con añadir sus yerros a los mios, sino con achacarme los agenos, pues sobre estar, como antes dixe (las ya no mias) llenas de erratas, y por el ahorro del papel, aun no cabales (pues donde acaba el pliego, acaba la Iornada, y donde acaba el quaderno, acaba la Comedia) hallè, ya adozenadas, y ya sueltas, todas estas que no son mias, impressas en mi nombre." There follows a list of 41 plays, published under the name of Calderón, which he does not acknowledge as his.

29. José M. Ruano de la Haza, "An Early Rehash of Lope's *Peribáñez*", *BCom*, 35 (1983), 5-29.

30. See note 28, above.

the case of that play at least, stage directions are truncated or omitted altogether in the printed version. It is necessary to bear this fact in mind when editing Court plays in particular.

A study of the manuscript of *Andrómeda y Perseo*, or of the description of Calderón's *Hado y divisa*[31], indicates another problem: what constitutes a stage direction? Early printed plays, such as those of Encina, appear to have stage directions, but, on examination, these often turn out to be descriptions of what took place on the one occasion for which the play was originally written; they are in the past tense, and not, as are the stage directions of seventeenth-century *comedias*, in the present tense. In other words, they are descriptive of the one occasion, and not intended to indicate to actors how the play is to be performed in the future. And the long stage directions which have been preserved for some Court plays, usually in manuscripts, but occasionally in the form of specially printed *sueltas*[32], are often descriptive, intended to convey the splendour of past royal occasions rather than to inform the actors in advance of rehearsal and performance.

In the nineteenth century many plays were reprinted, some for the first time since the seventeenth century, notably in the volumes of the *Biblioteca de Autores Españoles*. Nineteenth-century editors tended to regard the plays from the point of view of the more "realistic" settings of their day. Hartzenbusch, for instance, begins his edition of *El médico de su honra* with the following stage directions: "Vista externa de una quinta de Don Gutierre, inmediata a Sevilla. ESCENA PRIMERA" (347)[33]. As Don Enrique is brought on stage at line 26, Hartzenbusch begins "ESCENA II", even though line 26 is divided between the last speech in scene I and the first in scene II. He places a short printer's rule at the end of "ESCENA II", after line 44, and introduces a new stage direction: "Sala en la quinta de Don Gutierre. ESCENA III". The reader is therefore led to create in his mind's

---

31. Published by Juan Eugenio Hartzenbusch in *Comedias de D. Pedro Calderón de la Barca*, IV, *BAE* 14 (Madrid, 1945), 355-94.
32. Such as, for instance, the *suelta* studied by E.M. Wilson in "La edición principe de *Fieras afemina amor*, de don Pedro Calderón", *RBAM*, 24 (1955), 327-48.
33. Quotations are from *BAE*, 7, vol. I of the *Comedias de D. Pedro Calderón de la Barca*, ed. Juan Eugenio Hartzenbusch (Madrid, 1944).

eye a backdrop for scene I, also used for scene II, and to imagine a drop-scene or change of setting for scene III. That Hartzenbusch was fully conscious of what he was doing is shown by his footnote to *Los tres mayores prodigios*, in the same volume: "A semejanza de lo que hicimos en el tomo V de esta *Biblioteca*, se reimprime aquí una comedia de Calderón en la misma forma en que se publicó por primera vez, es decir, sin dividirla en escenas ni señalar los distintos lugares en que pasa la acción" (263). It is interesting to note that he appears to be making a distinction between the first publication of the play, which he clearly thinks primitive, and the practice of his own day. To what extent the introduction of "scenes" and the provision of "realistic" stage directions is influenced by contemporary practice outside Spain is a problem which has not, to my knowledge, been investigated, but Hartzenbusch's normal practice is, of course, in line with that of nineteenth-century editors of Shakespeare. Valbuena Briones, in his Clásicos Castellanos edition of *El médico de su honra*[34], has retained the Hartzenbusch stage directions, putting them in square brackets to indicate editorial intervention, but has suppressed the numbered scene divisions. However, his edition also leads the reader to suppose a much more "realistic" setting than was the reality of the seventeenth-century stage (13-15).

How, then, should the modern editor proceed? Ideally, the editor should work from the basis of a text known to have been composed with a particular theatre in mind, but he is seldom able to do so. Clearly, as with the spoken text of the play itself, the editor must go back to the autograph manuscript, if it exists; he must take into account the evidence of seventeenth-century printed texts, but remember that they may have been adulterated, and stage directions abridged or omitted for reasons of space; he must try and discover whether manuscripts other than the autograph are intended for staging conditions which differ from those originally intended by the author; and he must cast a very critical eye on nineteenth-century editions (and, alas, on many produced in this century also). Above all, he must bear in mind the

---

34. Pedro Calderón de la Barca, *Dramas de honor. II. El médico de su honra y El pintor de su deshonra*, ed. Angel Valbuena Briones, Clásicos Castellanos 142 (Madrid, 1965).

realities, as far as we are aware of them, of the staging conditions of the day.

* * *

Divisions within the acts of a play

Evidently, an act is usually conceived by the dramatist as divided into sections, which Ribbans has suggested should be called *cuadros*, a word less evocative of "scenery" than *escena*[35]. A *cuadro* ends when all the characters leave the stage, and another set of characters appear, thus indicating to the audience a change of location, also indicated to the audience by direct textual references, by the costumes worn by the actors, and by their method of acting. In the Tamesis Texts editions of *Peribáñez* and *El perro del hortelano*[36] the end of a *cuadro* is indicated by a plain rule, and the superfluous "scene" numbering is omitted. "Scenes" are unnecessary for reference purposes in plays written in verse, with constant line-numbering; in plays written in prose, or in a mixture of verse and prose, such as the plays of Shakespeare, "scene" numbering is more valid, since the content of a prose line depends on format. The Tamesis Texts lay-out represents a closer approach to staging conditions than the method employed by nineteenth-century editors, whilst clearly indicating the essential pauses in the action which signal to the audience the change of location.

Visualisation of the action

The editor must attempt to visualize the action of the play in the circumstances of its first production. In Act I of *El alcalde de Zalamea*, for instance, the Captain plans a means of getting up to the room in which Pedro Crespo's daughter is hidden: "Yo intento

35. G.W. Ribbans, "The Meaning and Structure of Lope's *Fuenteovejuna*", *BHS*, 31 (1954), 150-70.
36. Lope de Vega, *Peribáñez y el Comendador de Ocaña*, ed. J.M. Ruano and J.E. Varey (London, 1980); Lope de Vega, *El perro del hortelano*, ed. Victor Dixon (London, 1981).

/ subir a ese aposento / por ver si en él una persona habita, / que de mí hoy esconderse solicita" (636-40)[37]. He arranges to feign a quarrel with the soldier Rebolledo, and to pursue him upstairs. Chispa comments: "Que la espada ha sacado / el capitán para un soldado, / y, esa escalera arriba, / sube tras él" (675-78). It might appear logical, and more dramatic, that he would do so in the sight of the audience, but the text demonstrates that they leave the stage by a door at the rear, climb an inner staircase or ladder, and appear on the balcony from within the façade of the theatre building. Although the stage direction (681) does not so indicate, the subsequent action for the rest of Act I takes place on the balcony.

Missing stage directions

In the printed texts and in many manuscripts, it is evident that some stage directions are missing. Characters may clearly have left the stage, as indicated by the dialogue, without the stage direction: *Vase*. Other stage directions are sometimes indicated by the text as being necessary. In Act III of *El médico de su honra* the bloodless body of Doña Mencía is disclosed at line 824 in the discovery space. The King's following speech includes the lines: "Cubrid ese horror que asombra, / ese prodigio que espanta, / espectáculo que admira, / símbolo de la desgracia" (828-31). There is no stage direction to indicate when the curtains are drawn to, but it is evident that, apart from it being unusual for a King's order not to be obeyed, the dramatist would wish to draw the curtain in order that the ending of the play, with the ambiguous matching of Gutierre to Leonor, should not take place with the dead body in view. It would therefore be appropriate to introduce a stage direction: *Corren las cortinas*, before line 832. Any editorial intervention should, however, be indicated by the use of square brackets, parentheses being used for stage directions taken from the printed or manuscript source texts. The golden rule is to read the text with care, and follow the indications therein. New stage directions should therefore be added with circumspection.

37. Quotations are from Pedro Calderón de la Barca, *El alcalde de Zalamea*, ed. Peter N. Dunn (Oxford, 1966).

Format

Stage directions should be in italics. If long, they should be centered, and followed by a full-stop; if short, they can appear in the right-hand margin alongside the line of text to which they refer, in parentheses and without a full-stop. Short stage directions which directly affect the way in which a speech is delivered (e.g.: *Dentro; Aparte*) are usually placed in the verse immediately before the words affected:

PERIBANEZ: *[Ap.]* (Y mi deshonra también.)

As indicated, the aside itself should be in parentheses. Broken speeches should be indicated thus:

DONA MENCIA: Un hombre...
D. GUTIERRE: ¡Presto!
DONA MENCIA: ...escondido
en mi aposento he topado,
encubierto y rebozado.

Songs are best printed in italics, to establish their difference from the spoken dialogue. Lines should be indented where necessary to indicate verse patterns. The names of characters should be in small capitals, on the left of the text, and followed by a colon.

The line numbering should be consecutive throughout the text, and not be by acts. A line number should be given every five lines, and appear at the right of the text. Missing lines should be indicated by a row of dots.

Court plays

Plays performed at Court offer special difficulties, in that the discovery of the manuscript of *Andrómeda y Perseo* has shown how sparse the stage directions are in the printed text. The editor should therefore be on his guard, and look for indications of scene-changes in plays of spectacle. A particular problem arises from the fact that many Court plays use the same type of stage directions as are to be found in *corral* plays, e.g.: *Vase cada uno por su puerta: lo alto del teatro.* Sometimes the stage directions may lead the editor to suspect that what he has before him is a Court play rehashed for performance in the commercial theatres, or it may be that what has been generally taken to be a Court play is in effect a *corral* play. Calderón's two-part *La hija del aire* is a particularly difficult play to assess from this point of view. It has generally been taken to be a Court play, from a reference to it in the *Cuentas de la Cámara* in 1653[38]. Much recent work on this play has been directed to discussing whether the two parts of the play are by the same author, but the staging has been neglected, and a close examination of stage directions and text is clearly required. A reading of the two parts will clearly reveal the particular problems which the editor of a play intended for performance at Court must face.

* * *

Whilst the edition of a seventeenth-century play necessarily involves a close textual study of the variants of all editions and manuscripts in order to establish a *stemma*, and thus decide on the base text for the edition, the stage directions offer additional and specific problems. The above notes, it is hoped, will be of some assistance to future editors.

38. N.D. Shergold and J.E. Varey, "Some Early Calderón Dates", *BHS*, 38 (1961), 278-79.

NOTES ON THE CONTRIBUTORS

D.W. CRUICKSHANK was born in Kincardineshire, Scotland, in 1942. He attended Robert Gordon's College, Aberdeen, and the University of Aberdeen, where he studied Spanish under Terence May and Peter Dunn. After graduating in 1965, he moved to Cambridge, where he took his doctorate under the direction of Edward M. Wilson. In 1968 he was elected to a Research Fellowship at Emmanuel College, Cambridge; in 1970 he was appointed to a lectureship at University College, Dublin, where he became a Statutory Lecturer in Spanish in 1979. His interests include Golden Age Drama, European typography of the sixteenth and seventeenth centuries and fishing. He is married and has three children.

VICTOR F. DIXON is Professor of Spanish at Trinity College, Dublin. Born in London in 1932, he studied at Cambridge University, where he received the Ph.D. in 1959. He has taught at the University of St. Andrews and the University of Manchester and was a Visiting Associate Professor at Adelphi University in 1964-65. His publications include editions of Lope de Vega (?), *El sufrimiento premiado* (London, 1967) and Lope de Vega, *El perro del hortelano* (London, 1981) and sixteen articles on Golden Age dramatists. He has translated and directed three twentieth-century plays and has also directed and/or acted in over twenty productions in Spanish.

WILLIAM F. HUNTER was born in Aberdeen, Scotland, in 1941. After graduating from Aberdeen University, he did postgraduate research under E.M. Wilson at Cambridge University, where he was awarded the Ph.D. for an edition of Calderón's *auto La inmunidad del sagrario*. He now teaches at the University of Exeter. He has published an edition of the anonymous *auto La universal redención* and is Golden Age editor of Exeter Hispanic Texts.

The late ARNOLD G. REICHENBERGER was born in Karlsruhe, Germany, in 1903. He studied at the Universities of Heidelberg, Munich and Berlin, received his Doctorate in Classics from the University of Heidelberg in 1931. From 1934 to 1938 he was Lector in German at the University of Milan. He immigrated to the United States in 1939, teaching German and Italian at the New School for Social Research in New York during the academic year. During the following two years, he taught German and Latin at Capital University in Columbus, Ohio. He began his graduate studies of Spanish literature at Ohio University in 1942 and recieved the Ph.D. in 1946, at which time he was appointed an Instructor at the University of Pennsylvania, where he would continue to teach until his retirement. Promoted to Professor in 1961, he served as Chairman of his department from 1965 to 1967. He served on the editorial board of *Hispanic Review* from 1949 until he retired in 1973. Professor Reichenberger was a prolific scholar but is perhaps best remembered for his provocative article "The Uniqueness of the *Comedia*," published in *Hispanic Review* in 1959 and for his splendid critical editions of Lope de Vega's *Carlo V en Francia* (Pennsylvania, 1962) and *El preimero Benavides* (with Augusta Espantoso de Foley, Pennsylvania, 1973). Professor Reichenberger died on August 5, 1977.

JOHN E. VAREY is Professor of Spanish and Principal at Westfield College, University of London, where he has been teaching since 1952. Born in 1922, he studied at Cambridge University, completing his Ph.D. in 1951. He was a Visiting Professor at the University of Indiana in 1970-71 and at Purdue University in 1977. He was elected President of the ssociation of Hispanists of Great Britain and Ireland in 1979. He is General Editor of the Támesis Collection, joint editor of the series *Critical Guides to Spanish Texts* and *Research Bibliographies and Check-Lists*, and serves on the editorial boards of *Segismundo* and *Themes in Drama*. The author of numerous articles, he has also published editions of Tirso de Molina's *El burlador de Sevilla* (Cambridge, 1954; 2nd ed., 1967) and of Juan Vélez de Guevara's *Los celos hacen estrellas* (with N.D. Shergold and Jack Sage, London, 1970). He is presently preparing an edition of Calderón's *Las fortunas de Andrómeda y Perseo* in collaboration with Jack Sage. He is married and has three children.

VERN WILLIAMSEN is Professor of Spanish at the University of Missouri-Columbia, where he has been teaching since 1968. Born in California in 1926, he studied at San Jose Stage College and at the University of Arizona and received his Ph.D. from the University of Missouri in 1968. Professor Williamsen taught in elementary and secondary schools in California and Arizona from 1948 to 1965 and has also taught at Westminster College in Fulton, Missouri. His publications include editions of Mira de Amescua's *No hay dicha ni desdicha hasta la muerte* (Missouri, 1971) and *La casa del tahur* (Madrid, 1973), and Juan Ruiz de Alarcón's *Don Domingo de Don Blas* (Madrid, 1975), and *An Annotated, Analytical Bibliography of Tirso de Molina Studies* (Missouri, 1979). He is married and has two children.

di^spositio

Revista Hispánica de Semiótica Literaria

Vol. VII, No. 19-21; Winter-Spring, 1982

THE ART AND SCIENCE OF TRANSLATION

Guest Editors: André Lefevere and Kenneth David Jackson

Literary Theory and Translated Literature, André Lefevere; *A Rationale for Descriptive Translation Studies*, Gideon Toury; *The Conflict of Translation Models in France (end of 18th-Beginning 19th Century)*, Lieven D'hulst; *How Emile Deschamps Translated Shakespeare's MacBeth, or Theatre System and Translational System in French*, Jose Lambert; *The Tradition of a Translation and its Implications: 'The Vicar of Wakefield' in French Translation*, Katrin Van Bragt; *Cesare Pavese and America: The Myth of Translation and the Translation of Myth*, Cristina Bacchilega; *The Zodiac: Hendrick Marsman, Adriaan Barnouw, James Dickey (A Case Study in Interliterary Communication)*, Romy Heylen; *P. C. Hooft: The.Sonnets and the Tragedy*, Theo Hermans; *Texts and Contexts of Translation: A Dutch Classic in English*, Ria Vanderauwera; *Strategies for Integrating Irish Epics into European Literature*, Maria Tymoczko; *Translator as Refractor. Towards a Re-reading of James Clarence Mangan as Translator*, David Lloyd; *Walter Benjamin as Translation Theorist: A Reconsideration*, Marilyn Gaddis Rose; *Review: Gideon Toury In Search of a Theory of Translation*, Ria Vanderauwera; *Mephistofaustian Transluciferation (Contribution to the semiotics of poetic translation)*, Haroldo de Campos; *On Translating Haroldo de Campos*, Jean R. Longland; *The Pleasure of Subverting the Text: Oswald de Andrade's Seraphim Grosse Pointe*, Kenneth David Jackson; *In the Wake of the Word: Translating Guimaraes Rosa*, Stephanie Merrim; *On Translation and the Art of Repetition*, Alicia Borinsky; *Palimpsests. Trans-forms. and the Presence of the Original*, Fritz Hensey; *Two Ways of Translating Oral Poetry*, Hans C. ten Berg.

Vol. VIII, No. 22-23, 1983

RHETORIC IN THE HISPANIC WORLD
(XVI AND XVII CENTURIES)

An Introduction to the Study of Rhetoric in 16th Century Spain, Luisa López-Grigera; *La Retórica en Nueva España*, Ignacio Osorio Romero. *Hispanic Rhetorics in the XVI Century: A Bibliography*, D. Korn, D. Pollard et al; *Mateo Aleman's Voyage to a New World: The* Ortografia Castellana *of 1609*, Mark D. Johnston; *Intertextualidad, Interdiscursividad y Parodia: sobre los origenes de la forma narrativa en la novela picaresca*, Antonio Gómez-Moraiana; *La turbada historia de la palabra* ensayo, Manuel Alvar; *La Iconografía de Vicios y Virtudes en el Arte de Reinar de Guamn Poma de Ayala: Emblematica Politica al Servicio da una Tipologia Cultural Americana*, Mercedes López-Baralt. Reviews: *Philippe Hamon, Introduction à l'analyse du descriptif*, Ross Chambers; *Coextensiva Semantica Extensional del Texto*, Eduardo Forastieri Braschi.

Subscription, Manuscripts and Information:

Dispositio
Department of Romance Languages
University of Michigan
Ann Arbor, Michigan 48109

In Search of Eco's Roses

A special issue of *SubStance* devoted to Umberto Eco, with papers from THE NAME OF THE ROSE Colloquium held at the University of Texas at Austin. Issue #47 of *SubStance* also features an article by Eco and an essay by one of his translators.

Casablanca: Cult Movies and Intertextual Collage — Umberto Eco
Gaudy Rose: Eco and Narcissism — Teresa de Lauretis
The Name of the Book — Louis Mackey
Fear of Writing, or Adso and the Poisoned Text — Robert F. Yeager
The Invisible Worm: Ancients and Moderns in *The Name of the Rose* — Carl A. Rubino
The "Model Reader" and the Thermodynamic Model — Robert Artigiani
The Curious Case of Pharaoh's Polyp, and Related Matters — Douglass Parker
An Ethics of Significance — Leonard G. Schulze

AVAILABLE SEPTEMBER, 1985
Single Copies $6.95　One Year Subscription $15.00
(Institutions $30.00)
(Individuals please pre-pay)

Free Back Issue List and Detailed Brochure Available upon Request

Please remit to:　　**SubStance**
UW Press - Journals
114 N. Murray St.
Madison, WI 53715 USA
608-262-4952

ISSN 0049-2426　　Published Three Times Per Year　　Founded 1971
General Editors: Sydney Levy & Michel Pierssens
University of Wisconsin Press - Journals Division

REVUE FRANÇAISE D'ETUDES AMERICAINES

, rue Charles V - 75004 PARIS

A Journal published since 1976 by the French Association for American Studies (AFEA) A tri-annual from February 1982

°	1 April 1976	The Contemporary American Novel
°	2 October 1976	American Radicalism
°	3 April 1977	Civilization, Literature & Psychoanalysis, Littérature & Ideology
°	4 October 1977	American Humor
°	5 April 1978	Transcendentalism & the American Renaissance
°	6 October 1978	Ideology & the Mass Media in the US
°	7 April 1979	Arts & Society in the US
°	8 October 1979	Aspects of Modernity in the US
°	9 April 1980	Otherness in American Culture
°	10 October 1980	The Theaters of America
°	11 April 1981	The City in American Culture
°	12 October 1981	Religion in the US
°	13 February 1982	French Historians of the US
°	14 June 1982	Autobiography in America
°	15 November 1982	Contemporary American Poetry
°	16 February 1983	Intellectuals in the US
°	17 May 1983	American Writing in the Age of Realism
°	18 November 1983	North American English/Aspects of Translation
°	19 February 1984	Hollywood : Fact and Fiction
°	20 May 1984	Sex and Eroticism in American Literature
°	21 November 1984	The Economics of Powers in the US

. . . .

ill out and send to : RFEA, 10, rue Charles V - 75004 PARIS
ease - send........ copies of Nos 2, 3, 4, 5, 7, 8, 9, 10, 11, 12, 13, 14, 15, 16, 17, 18
 - enter my subscription for 19.....
AME : ....   * Price per issue : 45 FF (air mail)
DDRESS : ....   * One-year subscription :
....   — individuals : 120 FF
....   — institutions : 135 FF

RªJAH

The Rackham Journal of the Arts and Humanities
(RªJAH) is published by graduate students at the
University of Michigan.   RªJAH invites contributions from a wide range of disciplines, including
anthropology, history, political science, art history,
theatre, music, literary theory and the literatures
of all cultures. Contributors need not be students
from the University of Michigan.   RªJAH also
invites submissions of original photography and
art work.

Send manuscripts (S.A.S.E.) and correspondence to:

Editor, RªJAH
4024 Modern Languages Building
The University of Michigan
Ann Arbor, Michigan 48109

enjeux
revue de didactique du français

Rien ne va plus: faites vos (en)jeux!

C. Kerbrat-Orecchioni
Pour une approche pragmatique du dialogue théâtral

D. Lafontaine
«Oh, Monsieur Gaston, comme vous parlez bien!»
Une étude des variations sociolinguistiques dans *Gaston Lagaffe*

J. Blairon
Enjeux de la diversité
Analyse de *La Rempailleuse* de Maupassant (II)

J. Giot
La phonologie et les manuels scolaires (I)

H. Romian
A. Petitjean
Le point en didactique du français?

E. Charmeux
Construire une pédagogie efficace de l'écriture

J.-C. Meyer
J.-L. Phélut
Essai de généralisation d'un plan de formation à l'expression écrite au collège

Notes de lecture
E. Charmeux, *L'écriture à l'école*
(J.-P. Laurent)
J.-C. Meyer et J.-L. Phélut,
Apprendre à écrire le français au collège
(I. Legros)

Prix	Belgique	Etranger
Abonnement annuel (par année scolaire)	750 FB	850 FB
Le numéro	300FB	325FB

Les demandes sont reçues aux Editions LABOR
Rue Royale, 324 - B-1030 BRUXELLES

CEDOCEF
FACULTES UNIVERSITAIRES DE NAMUR

EDITIONS
LABOR-NATHAN

REVUE FRANÇAISE D'ETUDES AMERICAINES

rue Charles V - 75004 PARIS

A Journal published since 1976 by the French
Association for American Studies (AFEA)
A tri-annual from February 1982

1 April 1976	The Contemporary American Novel
2 October 1976	American Radicalism
3 April 1977	Civilization, Literature & Psychoanalysis, Littérature & Ideology
4 October 1977	American Humor
5 April 1978	Transcendentalism & the American Renaissance
6 October 1978	Ideology & the Mass Media in the US
7 April 1979	Arts & Society in the US
8 October 1979	Aspects of Modernity in the US
9 April 1980	Otherness in American Culture
10 October 1980	The Theaters of America
11 April 1981	The City in American Culture
12 October 1981	Religion in the US
13 February 1982	French Historians of the US
14 June 1982	Autobiography in America
15 November 1982	Contemporary American Poetry
16 February 1983	Intellectuals in the US
17 May 1983	American Writing in the Age of Realism
18 November 1983	North American English/Aspects of Translation
19 February 1984	Hollywood : Fact and Fiction
20 May 1984	Sex and Eroticism in American Literature
21 November 1984	The Economics of Powers in the US

. . . .

ill out and send to : RFEA, 10, rue Charles V - 75004 PARIS

lease - send........ copies of Nos 2, 3, 4, 5, 7, 8, 9, 10, 11, 12, 13, 14, 15, 16, 17, 18
   - enter my subscription for 19.....

AME : ....

DDRESS : ....

....

....

* Price per issue : 45 FF (air mail)
* One-year subscription :
   — individuals : 120 FF
   — institutions : 135 FF